Creative DOLL CRAFT

GLORIA McKINNON

A J.B. Fairfax Press Publication

CONTENTS

ACKNOWLEDGMENTS

My very special thanks go to Wendy Lee Ragan and Susan York, my American friends, who are always there when needed. Thanks also go to Sue McNeill of New Zealand, another valued member of the Anne's Glory Box family.

And, of course, at home, special thanks to Fay King, my store manager; Marg Manning; Anne Riseborough and Colleen Potts.

Gloria McKinnon

EDITORIAL
Managing Editor: Judy Poulos
Editorial Assistant: Ella Martin
Editorial Coordinator: Margaret Kelly

PHOTOGRAPHY
Andrew Payne
Styling: Anne-Maree Unwin

ILLUSTRATIONS
Maggie Cooper, Lesley Griffith

DESIGN AND PRODUCTION
Design: Jenny Nossal
Cover Design: Jenny Pace, Jenny Nossal
Managers: Sheridan Carter, Anna Maguire
Picture Editor: Kirsten Holmes
Layout: Maggie Cooper

Published by J.B. Fairfax Press Pty Limited
80-82 McLachlan Ave
Rushcutters Bay, Australia 2011
A.C.N. 003 738 430

Formatted by J.B. Fairfax Press Pty Limited

Printed by Toppan Printing Co. Hong Kong
© J.B. Fairfax Press Pty Limited 1995

JBFP 402

CREATIVE DOLL CRAFT
ISBN 1 86343 236 1

CONTENTS

FOREWORD

Dolls have come a long way since cavemen carved small playthings from wood and bone. We all treasure memories of special birthdays or Christmases, when we unwrapped the tissue paper from that first special doll and wondered at her shiny curls and pursed lips.

This love of dolls has remained with many of us into adulthood, blossoming into creative expression through dollmaking or dressmaking. Dollmaking has certainly evolved from those rudimentary playthings. These days, experienced doll artists, working in their studios, create wonderful dolls in the style of French and German antiques, as well as designing modern dolls of equal beauty. These studios also serve as classrooms for the thousands of aspiring doll artists. Once made, these dolls are lovingly dressed in clothes appropriate to their period and style.

In this book you will find patterns and instructions for making beautiful dresses, underwear, jackets and more. Each garment is designed with an eye towards detail and style, but each one is quite simple for an average sewer to make.

A less formal, though equally popular, form of dollmaking is that of cloth dollmaking. This traditional craft continues to evolve with many dollmakers revelling in the ready availability of interesting and unusual fabrics to extend their craft. In the following pages, you will find some charming cloth dolls to make, each one an individual.

Whether you are a dollmaker in the classic tradition, a collector of antique dolls or a lover of cloth dolls, you will find something to please you in this book. All the designs are suitable for beginners, but there are also some special techniques to challenge the more experienced.

DRESSING DOLLS

Dressmaking for dolls is very satisfying. On a
reduced scale, you can create 'real' clothes that would be
expensive and time-consuming to make in a normal size.

You can afford to use special fabric scraps which you might not find a use for otherwise or expensive trims. If you are an embroiderer, you will find dressmaking for dolls a wonderful outlet for your creativity.

SETTING THE STYLE

Dolls, like people, come in a variety of shapes and sizes. Choose a style of dress that is appropriate to your doll. A bridal outfit would not sit well on a baby doll, nor would a christening gown look appropriate on a lady doll.

Many dolls are also clearly identified with a certain period: antique, antique reproduction or modern. Choose a style of dress, wig and accessories that are appropriate to the period.

If you are dressing your doll for a competition, it is particularly important to pay attention to these details. For example, there was no nylon lace before the 1950s, nor did the colour orange ever appear on the dolls we now call antique, so their reproduction versions should follow these conventions. Underwear for these dolls should always be white.

CHOOSING THE FABRIC

As with most needlework, choose the very best materials that you can afford and that suit your particular project. Natural fibres, such as fine cotton voile, silk and wool, are ideal for doll dressmaking. They are generally easier to work with, and drape and shape better than most synthetics. Some modern synthetic silk-like fabrics are good and can be substituted for the real thing, but not for competition.

Pay attention to colour and print when choosing fabric for a doll's outfit. Bold stripes which look dramatic on you will simply overwhelm a 30 cm (12 in) doll. In general, small prints are best for dolls.

When it comes to colour, follow the same rules as you would for choosing your own clothes – to complement hair colour, eye colour and complexion. If you can't take the doll shopping with you, take home some fabric swatches to see what suits the doll best.

If you are dressing an antique doll, it is wonderful if you can use 'antique' fabric, even if it is only a tiny piece for a collar. Grandmother's sewing box, the church bazaar or the local op-shop are all good sources of old fabrics. Making small pieces for dolls also means that you need relatively little fabric which you can often recycle from an existing garment. Keep an eye out for old evening clothes, silk nighties and lace blouses – they are great sources of fabric. Table linen and handkerchiefs, particularly if they are from fine linen, are also very useful.

Naturally, there are many beautiful new fabrics which are very suitable for dressing dolls.

THE RIGHT TRIM

Many of the garments in this book have been trimmed with a variety of laces: insertion laces, beading and lace edging of various widths. As a general rule, always choose cotton lace. French laces which are marked ninety per cent cotton and ten per cent nylon are classed as cotton laces. Nylon laces do not usually work well, except for fantasy dolls. For an antique or a good reproduction doll, choose the very best lace you can afford from the huge variety which is available in the stores. You will usually not need to buy very much and the finished result will be worth the expense.

If you would rather use cream lace but cannot find one you like, it is not difficult to dye white lace to a lovely cream colour, using tea. Wet a length of lace, then dip it into a cup of tea. If you are happy with the colour, add two teaspoons of white vinegar to the cup and dip the lace again to set the colour. If the colour is too light or too dark, you can adjust the strength of the solution. When you have dyed in this way a couple of times, you will be confident enough to judge the colour and add the vinegar right at the beginning, but until then it is a good idea to have a trial run. When you have dyed all the lace you need, allow it to dry naturally (not in the clothes dryer), then iron it.

Ribbons and braids are also popular trimmings for dolls clothes. As with lace, there is a huge range from which to choose.

Tiny brooches, beads, embroidered motifs and silk or dried flowers are all very suitable for dolls. Take care when choosing trims that they are compatible with the style of the dress and not likely to 'drown' it. A dainty hat with an overly large flower can look more suitable for a clown than for an elegant doll!

USING THE PATTERNS

Each pattern in this book is identified by the size of the doll which it suits and this size is always given as the height of the doll. Height on its own is not an infallible guide, however. A lady doll is likely to be more slender than a child doll of the same height and will have slimmer arms and legs. It is always best to measure your doll and check those measurements against the pattern. Once you have measured your doll, it is quite a simple matter to alter a pattern to suit. Measure all the areas indicated in figure 1, using a tape measure. For awkward or very small measurements, use a piece of tape or string, then check the length on the tape measure. Once you have taken the measurements, put them away for a particular doll, you can use them again and again because, unlike people, dolls do not change their shape!

Check your measurements against the pattern you have chosen. Note that all the patterns are given full size with seam allowances and an additional allowance for ease included. This additional allowance is particularly important when it comes to actually slipping the dress on the doll. Will the dress pass over her head? Will the sleeves pass over her hands? Will the feet pass through the leg of her pants?

It is a good idea to trace the patterns onto tissue paper or, preferably, Vilene to make a toile. Do not cut them out at this stage. Mark all your alterations on the tracing, then cut out the pattern pieces around the new outline. Pin the pieces onto the doll to check the fit. Alter any markings as necessary then use these pattern pieces to cut the fabric. Label this toile with the name of the doll, then store it away for future use.

Making a toile might seem like an awful lot of trouble, but it will save you a lot of disappointment later, especially if you are using a precious piece of antique silk.

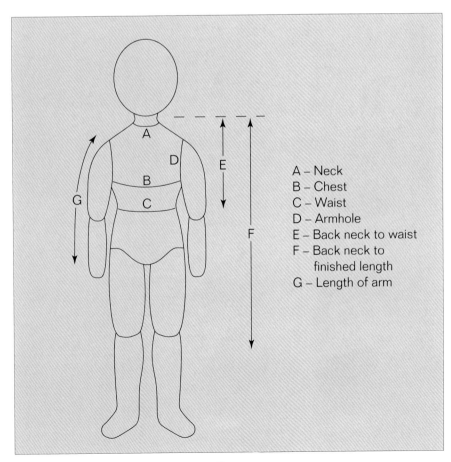

A – Neck
B – Chest
C – Waist
D – Armhole
E – Back neck to waist
F – Back neck to finished length
G – Length of arm

Fig. 1

7

STITCH GUIDE

EMBROIDERY TECHNIQUES

SATIN STITCH

Satin stitch is most commonly used to fill in a given area with straight stitches placed very close together. Keep your stitches very even to give a smooth finish.

FRENCH KNOT

French knots are ideal for flower centres. Begin by bringing the needle up through the fabric where you wish the knot to sit. Wrap the thread twice around the needle, then reinsert the needle close to where it emerged, gently pulling the thread taut (Fig. 1). Bring the needle out at the position of the next French knot (Fig. 2).

STEM STITCH

Stem stitch is commonly used for outlines and for the stems of flowers. Simply take a long stitch, bringing the needle out approximately half a stitch length back (Fig. 3). Repeat this procedure along the desired length, keeping the thread below the needle (Fig. 4).

LAZY DAISY STITCH

For lazy daisy stitch, bring the needle up through the fabric at the point where you wish to place the centre of the flower. Leaving a loop, take the needle back through the fabric close to the point where it emerged. Secure the loop with a tiny stitch across the end, then bring the needle back up through the centre ready to make the next petal (Fig. 5).

BULLION STITCH

Bullion stitches are used either on their own or in groups to create roses.

To make a bullion stitch, bring the needle up through the fabric at **a**, then take a stitch back to **b**, bringing the point of the needle out again at **a** without pulling it right through (Fig. 6).

Wrap the thread around the needle five times (or the number stated in the instructions). Pull the needle through, gently guiding the wraps off the needle onto the fabric. Reinsert the needle at **b** to secure the bullion (Fig. 7).

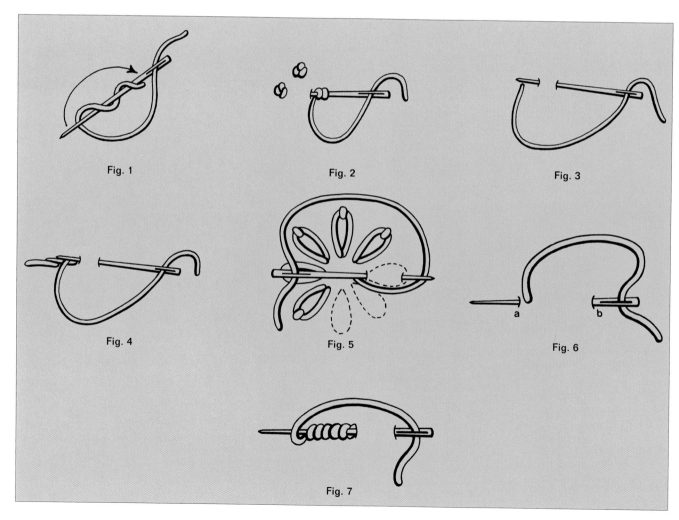

Fig. 1

Fig. 2

Fig. 3

Fig. 4

Fig. 5

Fig. 6

Fig. 7

To make a bullion rosebud, lay two bullion stitches (one slightly longer than the other) side by side.

To make a simple bullion rose, lay three bullion stitches (the middle one is usually two wraps shorter than the two outside ones) side by side.

SHADOW EMBROIDERY

For shadow embroidery, you create a basketweave of thread which covers the area to be filled.

Begin by bringing the needle through at **a** and take a stitch to **b**, bringing the needle out at **c**. Take a stitch to **b** (Fig. 8).

Bring the needle out at **d** and take a stitch to **a**. On the wrong side, carry the thread over, bringing it out at **e** and take stitch to **c** (Fig. 9).

On the wrong side, carry the thread over, bringing it out at **f**, then take a stitch back to **d**. On the wrong side, carry the thread over, bringing

it out at **g**, then take a stitch back to **e** (Fig. 10).

Continue in this way until the entire area is filled.

HEIRLOOM SEWING TECHNIQUES

PINSTITCH

Pinstitching is a decorative way of attaching laces to fabric. It is very simple to do by machine, if you can use a wing needle on your sewing machine. The following steps are for pinstitching by hand.

Working from right to left, bring the needle through from the back of the work at **a**, make a backstitch to **b**, then pull the thread through to the back of the work. Bring the needle back up through the fabric to **c** which is directly below **a**. The needle will be pointing

diagonally from **b** to **c** (Fig. 11).

Take a stitch from **c** to **a**, pulling the thread through to the back, then bring the needle up through **d**. Backstitch to **a** (Fig. 12). Tugging the thread slightly as you work horizontally will open up the holes in the fabric, giving it a very light entredeux look.

ROLLING AND WHIPPING

This technique is commonly used to prepare fabric for joining to lace. It works best on a straight edge.

With the wrong side of the fabric facing you and working from right to left, place a needle just below the top edge and begin to roll the top edge over the needle, using your left hand. It can be helpful to moisten the fingers doing the rolling (Fig. 13).

Continue to roll the fabric in this way until the raw edge has completely disappeared, remove the needle and go on rolling. This will be easier to

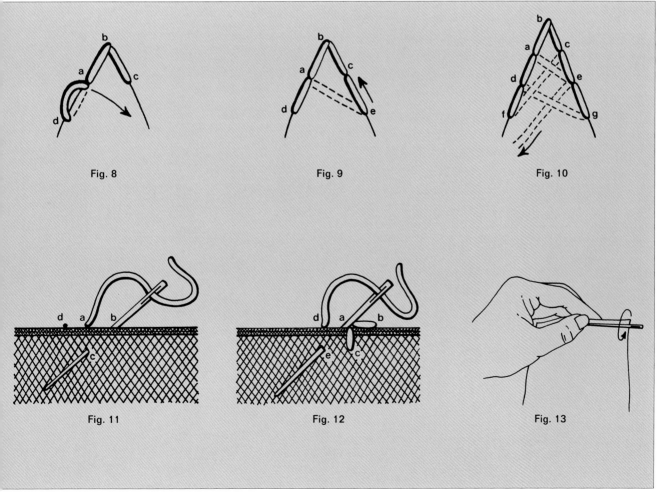

Fig. 8   Fig. 9   Fig. 10

Fig. 11   Fig. 12   Fig. 13

achieve if you keep the fabric quite taut between your hands as you roll.

When you have completed approximately 25 cm (10 in), begin to stitch over the roll with a whipstitch. To whip the edge you have just rolled or to add lace, pass the needle under the roll, bringing it out on the edge, then pass the needle over the roll ready to repeat the stitch. If you are attaching lace, pick up the edge of the lace into your stitching. Try to keep your stitches small and even (Fig. 14).

PINTUCKING

Pintucks are usually stitched on the straight grain of the fabric. Pintucks can be stitched quite simply using a pintucking foot on your sewing machine. This foot forms the tucks automatically as you sew. Press all the tucks in the same direction.

FRENCH SEAMS

Place the fabrics together with the wrong sides facing. Stitch the seam, then trim the seam allowance back to 3 mm (1/8 in).

Fold the fabric so that the right sides are facing and stitch the seam again, enclosing the previous seam allowance. Press the seam to one side.

LACE SHAPING

To shape lace around a curve, pin the outside edge of the lace around the curve (Fig. 15).

Pull the thread on the inside edge of the lace heading to gather it, then pin this edge in place (Fig. 16). Straight stitch through both lace headings.

On the wrong side, slash the fabric between the lines of stitching, then clip the fabric so it will fold back neatly (Fig. 17). Fold and press the fabric back exposing the lace.

On the right side, zigzag over the heading and the folded fabric. Trim away any excess fabric (Fig. 18).

JOINING TWO STRAIGHT EDGES OF LACE

Spray starch both pieces of lace. Place them side by side so the edges are butted together but not overlapping. Try to match the patterns in the lace for the best effect. Beginning 6 mm (1/4 in) from the ends of the lace, zigzag the edges together, using a stitch just wide enough to catch the headings of both laces. Choose a stitch length that you think looks best – neither a satin stitch nor one so long that the laces are not held together properly.

JOINING A FLAT LACE EDGE TO ENTREDEUX

Trim the batiste from one side of the entredeux. Spray starch the lace and the entredeux. With both right sides facing upwards, place the lace and the

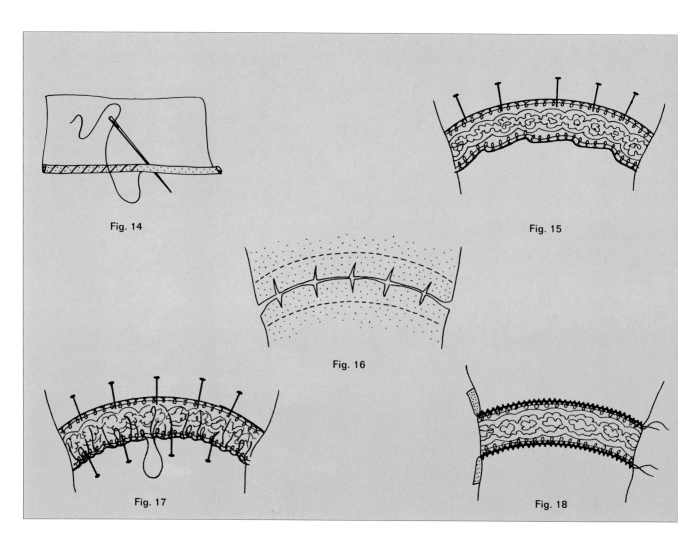

Fig. 14

Fig. 15

Fig. 16

Fig. 17

Fig. 18

trimmed edge of the entredeux butted together but not overlapping. Zigzag them together with a stitch length and width that places the needle into one hole of the entredeux on the 'zig' and then just over the heading of the lace on the 'zag' (Fig. 19). You won't be able to achieve this every time, but try to set your machine as close as possible to this pattern.

JOINING A FLAT LACE EDGE TO FABRIC

Spray starch and press the fabric and the lace. Place the lace and the fabric together, with the right sides facing so the fabric extends about 3 mm (¹/₈ in) beyond the lace (Fig. 20).

Zigzag with a satin stitch so the needle goes into the heading of the lace on the 'zig' and all the way off the fabric on the 'zag' (Fig. 21). This method rolls the raw edge right into the stitch as you go. Not only does this method give a better finish, if you join the lace and fabric edge-to-edge, they will come apart.

JOINING ENTREDEUX TO FLAT FABRIC

(Stitch-in-the-ditch method)

Do not trim the entredeux. Spray starch and press the fabric and the entredeux. Place the batiste edge of the entredeux and the fabric edge together, with the right sides facing. Stitch along the side of the entredeux closest to the body of the sewing machine, using a short straight stitch. You are stitching 'in the ditch' of the entredeux (Fig. 22).

Using a tight zigzag about 6 mm (¹/₄ in) wide, but not a satin stitch, stitch over the seam you have just sewn (Fig. 23). Trim away the excess batiste (Fig. 24).

Press the seam towards the fabric. All the holes of the entredeux should now be visible.

Working on the right side of the fabric, zigzag into one hole of the entredeux, then just barely into the fabric (Fig. 25). Adjust your stitch length and width to achieve this.

JOINING ENTREDEUX TO GATHERED FABRIC

Press the fabric. Do not trim the entredeux. Pin the gathered fabric to the entredeux. Stitch, following the directions for joining entredeux to flat fabric. The final step may be easier to do with the wrong side up because of the bulk of the seam.

GATHERING FRENCH LACE BY HAND

Cut a length of lace two or three times the finished length. Gather up the lace by pulling one of the heavy threads running along the straight edge. Adjust the gathers evenly and check the length before attaching the lace.

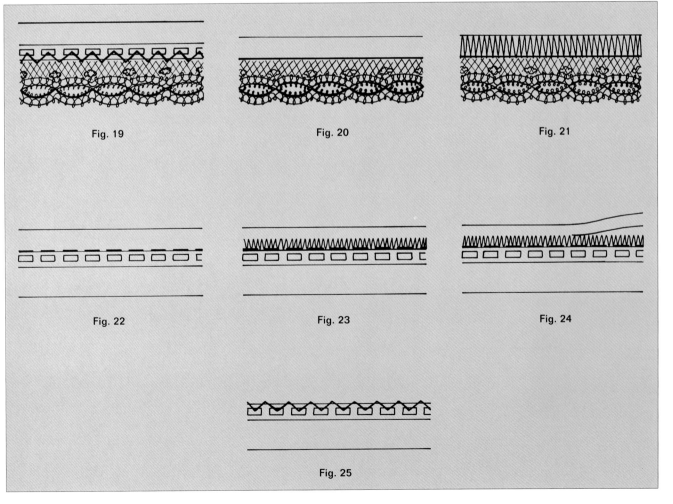

Fig. 19   Fig. 20   Fig. 21

Fig. 22   Fig. 23   Fig. 24

Fig. 25

MAKING CLOTH DOLLS

**Soft and reassuring companions of childhood, cloth dolls
retain a warm spot in the hearts of many adults.**

Whether prompted by these remembered pleasures or by the opportunity for creativity, cloth dollmaking is an increasingly popular art form. As with most other creative endeavours, most dollmakers begin with a given pattern. The three cloth dolls in this book are all very different and each one offers the opportunity to further develop the pattern.

MATERIALS

Requirements are very simple for making cloth dolls. Apart from your basic sewing supplies, you will need a suitable cream or flesh-coloured fabric for the body (homespun or osnaburg is ideal); fabric for the clothing; paints for facial features; and material for making the hair (bought curls, wool, hemp or a wig). Not all cloth dolls have hair, some have just the suggestion of hair while others, like Tatiana on page 68, have no hair at all.

PATTERNS

The patterns given in this book should be traced onto tracing or tissue paper, then transferred to the wrong side of the fabric. Pattern pieces are joined with the right sides facing, leaving an opening for stuffing. If the face is to be embroidered or painted, read the instructions to see if this should be done before or after the doll is assembled.

CREATING THE FACE

A variety of paints are suitable for cloth dolls including fabric paints, artists' acrylic paints, permanent markers and even watercolours, as long as you use a fixative.

Study the photograph of the doll's face given in the book and practise your strokes or lines on a scrap of fabric before you begin. It is important that you approach the task confidently so your lines are crisp and clean. Begin by roughing in the eyes, then the nose and mouth to get the proportions right, then begin painting in the same order.

Doll's faces can also be embroidered with simple straight and satin stitches. Some dollmakers use a combination of paint and embroidery to achieve the look they want.

STUFFING THE DOLL

Some cloth dolls are completed before stuffing, others are stuffed bit by bit as you go along. How you stuff your doll is crucial to the final outcome. The doll should have no lumps or empty spots. The stuffing should be firm but not so hard as to make the doll unyielding to touch. The best stuffings to use are washable polyester, available in bag lots. Do not use foam chips or cut-up pantyhose – the effect will be disappointing and will detract from your doll.

Begin by inserting small pinches of stuffing, using a chopstick or something similar to push the stuffing into the hard-to-get-at corners. Keep adding only small amounts of stuffing at a time, working from the extremities towards the centre of the body. Mould and flatten with your hands as you go.

CAROLINE

By Sue McNeill

**Looking charming in cream batiste
trimmed with lace and pintucks, Caroline
catches up on her reading.**

This dress has been hand-sewn, but you can use machine-sewing, if you prefer.

SIZE

To fit a 56 cm (22 in) doll

MATERIALS

80 cm (31½ in) of 115 cm (45 in) wide Swiss batiste
3 m (3¼ yd) of 15 mm (⅝ in) wide insertion lace
1 m (1⅛ yd) of 12 mm (½ in) wide beading
2 m (2¼ yd) of 15 mm (⅝ in) wide lace edging
2.5 m (2¾ yd) of 3 mm (⅛ in) wide entredeux
2 m (2¼ yd) of 4 mm (³⁄₁₆ in) wide silk ribbon
Five 7 mm (⁵⁄₁₆ in) buttons
Embroidery threads
Needles for sewing and for embroidery
Tracing or tissue paper
Fineline permanent marker pen
Water-soluble pen or pencil
Matching sewing thread
Small sharp scissors

BEFORE YOU BEGIN

See the patterns, the lace placement guides and the embroidery designs on pages 18-20. All the seams are 6 mm (¼ in) unless otherwise stated.

Trace all the patterns onto the tissue or tracing paper, using the marker pen.

Draw a thread on the Swiss batiste to find the straight grain before cutting out the frills and the skirt.

Read all the instructions and the section on dressing dolls beginning on page 6.

CONSTRUCTION

FOR THE FRONT BODICE

STEP ONE

Using the pattern provided, cut out the front bodice section **B** on the fold. Transfer all the markings and the lace placement guide onto the fabric with the water-soluble pen or pencil.

STEP TWO

Using the lace placement guide, measure out two lengths of insertion lace, marking the mitres. Stitch the mitres and press. Pin, then baste the insertion lace into place with tiny running stitches. Split the fabric behind the lace with the small scissors, taking care not to cut the lace. Fold the fabric back to the lace edge and pinstitch along both edges of the lace and fabric. Trim away any excess fabric.

STEP THREE

Fold the pintucks along the solid lines. Stitch seven pintucks on each side, stitching 1 mm (¹⁄₃₂ in) from the fold, using tiny running stitches or by machine. (See page 10 for tips on pintucking.) Press the tucks away from the centre of the bodice.

STEP FOUR

Transfer all the markings and the lace placement guide onto the front yoke **A** with the water-soluble pen or pencil. Using the lace placement guide, measure out a length of insertion lace, marking the mitres. Stitch the mitres and press. Using the pattern provided, cut out the front yoke.

STEP FIVE

Pin, then stitch the insertion lace into place with tiny running stitches. Split the fabric behind the lace, taking care not to cut the lace. Fold the fabric back to the lace edge and pinstitch along the top edge of the lace. Trim away any excess fabric.

STEP SIX

Pin, then stitch the lower edge of the lace to the front bodice. Check the full bodice and yoke you have now constructed against the full pattern piece to make sure everything is lined up. Fold the seam allowance behind the lace back to the lace edge. Pinstitch along the lower edge. Trim away any excess fabric and press.

STEP SEVEN

Transfer the flower design from the pattern onto the front bodice with the water-soluble pen or pencil. Embroider the design in the stitches and embroidery threads indicated.

FOR THE BACK BODICE

STEP ONE

Using the pattern provided, cut out the back bodice **D** and attach the insertion lace in the same way as for the front bodice.

STEP TWO

Using the pattern provided, cut out the back yoke **C** and attach the lace in the same way as for the front yoke.

STEP THREE

To attach the back yoke to the back bodice, gather the top edge of the back bodice with tiny running stitches. Pin, then stitch the lower edge of the lace on the back yoke to the gathered edge with tiny running stitches. Check the piece against the full pattern as before. Fold the fabric back to the lace edge. Pinstitch along the lace edge. Trim away any excess fabric.

STEP FOUR

For the back openings, fold the edges to the inside along both fold lines. Pinstitch, then press, as before.

STEP FIVE

Join the shoulders with small French seams. Press.

FOR THE NECKLINE

STEP ONE

Cut a 19 cm (7½ in) length of beading. Pin, then stitch the beading around the neck on the seam line. Fold the seam allowance back to the lace edge. Pinstitch around the edge, then trim away any excess fabric.

STEP TWO

Cut a 30.5 cm (12 in) length of lace edging. Gather the edging to fit the beading around the neckline. Whip-

stitch the two together. Turn in the raw ends of the lace even with the back opening and hand-sew them in place.

FOR THE SLEEVES

STEP ONE

Using the pattern provided, cut two pieces of fabric 21 cm x 10 cm (8¼ in x 4 in) for the sleeve heads. On each piece, fold the longer sides in half. Stitch a pintuck on the fold as on the front bodice, then stitch three more pintucks on either side. Press.

STEP TWO

Place the sleeve head pattern **E** on the pintucked pieces and cut out two sleeve heads, marking the front and back, and taking care to cut a right and a left sleeve.

STEP THREE

Measure a length of insertion lace for each sleeve head and mark the mitres. Stitch the mitres, then press.

STEP FOUR

Using the sleeve pattern **F**, cut out the bottom part of the sleeves. Mark the centre, front and back. Place the sleeve head and the lower sleeve section on the full sleeve pattern. Mark the placement lines for the lace.

STEP FIVE

Pin the insertion lace on the marked lines, then stitch with tiny running stitches. Slit the fabric behind the lace and fold the fabric back to the lace edge. Pinstitch along the lace edge. Trim away any excess fabric. Press.

STEP SIX

Transfer the sleeve embroidery design, using the water-soluble pen or pencil. Embroider the design using the stitches and threads indicated.

STEP SEVEN

Roll and whip along the bottom edge of the sleeves to gather them. For each sleeve cut a 12 cm (4¾ in) length of entredeux. Trim the fabric from one edge of the entredeux. Gather the sleeve ends to fit the entredeux. Whip stitch the sleeve ends and the entredeux together. Cut a length of beading and whipstitch it to the entredeux. Cut another length of entredeux and whipstitch it to the beading.

STEP EIGHT

For each frill, cut a 3 cm x 25 cm (1¼ in x 10 in) piece of fabric and a piece of lace edging the same length. Pin, baste and pinstitch the lace to one long side of the fabric. Roll and whip the other long side to gather it to fit the entredeux at the bottom edge of the sleeve. Whipstitch the gathered frill to the entredeux.

STEP NINE

Gather the sleeve heads with tiny running stitches. Pin the sleeves into the armholes, matching fronts and backs and placing the centre mark to the shoulder seams. Stitch the sleeves in place. Press.

TO COMPLETE THE BODICE

STEP ONE

Join the side and the underarm seams in one go, using French seams.

STEP TWO

Gather the bottom edge of the bodice with tiny running stitches. Overlap the left back over the right back, matching centres. Cut a 37 cm (14½ in) length of entredeux. Do not trim away the fabric from the edges. Divide the length of entredeux equally into quarters, overlapping the ends at the centre back. Gather up the bottom edge of the bodice to fit the entredeux. Pin, then stitch the entredeux to the bodice, stitching in the channel of the entredeux and matching centres. Trim the seam and neaten the edges.

STEP THREE

Trim the fabric from the lower edge of the entredeux. Cut a 37 cm (14½ in) length of beading. Seam the ends together, then whipstitch the beading to the entredeux, placing the ends at the centre back. Cut another length of trimmed entredeux to match and whipstitch it to the beading.

FOR THE SKIRT

STEP ONE

Cut a piece of fabric 9 cm x 76 cm (3½ in x 30 in). Fold up 2.5 cm (1 in) along one long side. This is the skirt hem line and the position of the first pintuck. Make the first pintuck on the fold, the second one 6 mm (¼ in) up, and the third pintuck 6 mm (¼ in) up from the second one. Press all the pintucks down.

STEP TWO

Cut a 76 cm (30 in) length of insertion lace. Pin, then stitch the lace to the lower edge of the skirt in the hem allowance. Fold the seam back to the lace edge. Pinstitch along the lace edge. Trim away the excess fabric.

STEP THREE

Join the skirt centre back with a small French seam.

STEP FOUR

Cut a 76 cm (30 in) length of entredeux and whipstitch it to the insertion lace. Trim the lower edge of the entredeux. Press. Divide and mark the length of the entredeux into quarters.

STEP FIVE

Cut a 6.5 cm x 108 cm (2½ in x 42½ in) piece of fabric for the frill. Cut a piece of lace edging the same length. Pin, then stitch the lace edging to one long side of the frill on the seam allowance. Fold the seam back to the lace edge. Pinstitch along the edge. Trim away any excess fabric. Join the ends of the frill with a French seam.

STEP SIX

Roll and whip the top edge of the frill to gather it. Divide the frill into quarters. Gather the length of the frill to fit the entredeux. Pin the frill to the entredeux, matching the quarter points on

Pintucking and lace insertion work well together

the top part of the skirt, then whipstitch them together. Press.

TO COMPLETE THE DRESS

STEP ONE

Trim the top edge of the skirt so that the finished length is 16 cm (6¼ in). Divide the top edge of the skirt into quarters. Roll and whip the top edge of the skirt to gather it. Pin the skirt to the entredeux on the bottom of the bodice, matching quarter points, then whipstitch them together.

STEP TWO

Hand-sew five buttonholes down the back opening. Sew on the buttons to correspond.

STEP THREE

Cut two 40 cm (15¾ in) lengths of silk ribbon. Thread them through the beading on the sleeves, then tie the ends into bows. Cut two 25 cm (10 in) lengths of silk ribbon for the neck. Hand-sew one end of each ribbon at the back, thread the ribbons through the beading, then tie them in a bow at the front. Thread the remaining ribbon through the beading at the waist.

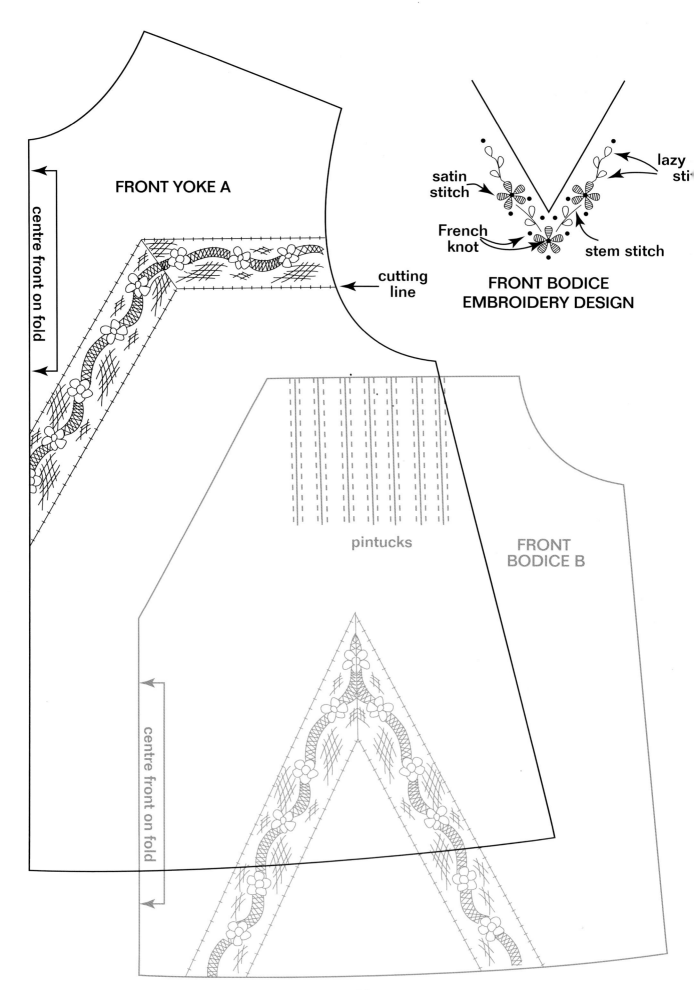

FRONT YOKE A

centre front on fold

cutting line

satin stitch

lazy stitch

French knot

stem stitch

FRONT BODICE EMBROIDERY DESIGN

pintucks

FRONT BODICE B

centre front on fold

18

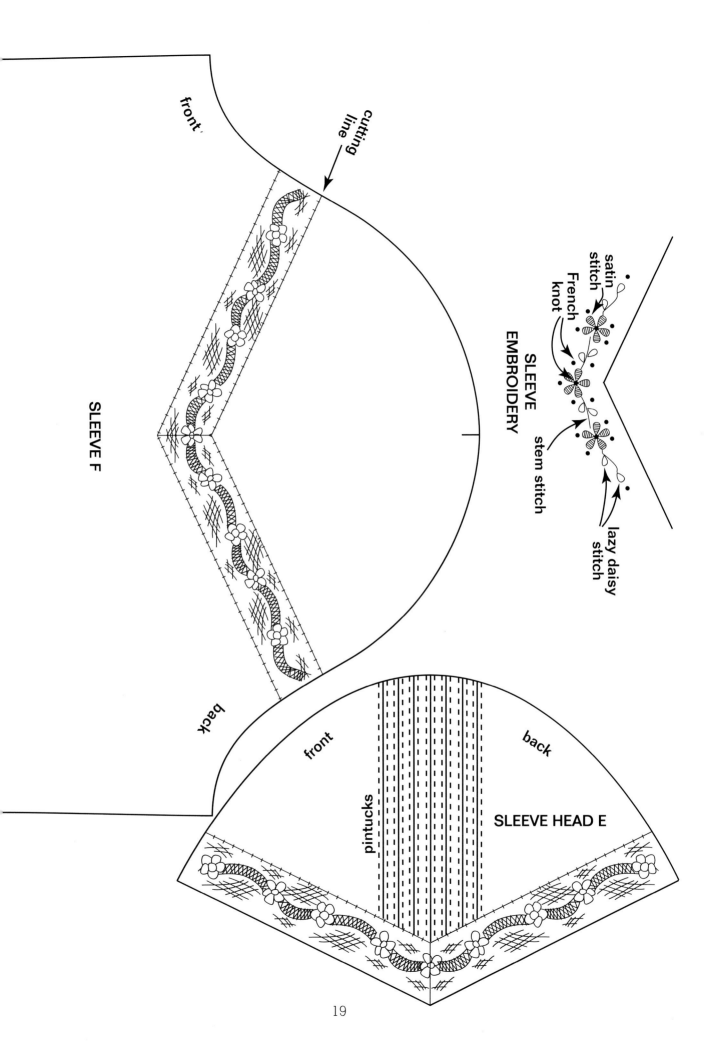

SLEEVE F

front

cutting line

back

SLEEVE EMBROIDERY

satin stitch

French knot

stem stitch

lazy daisy stitch

SLEEVE HEAD E

front

back

pintucks

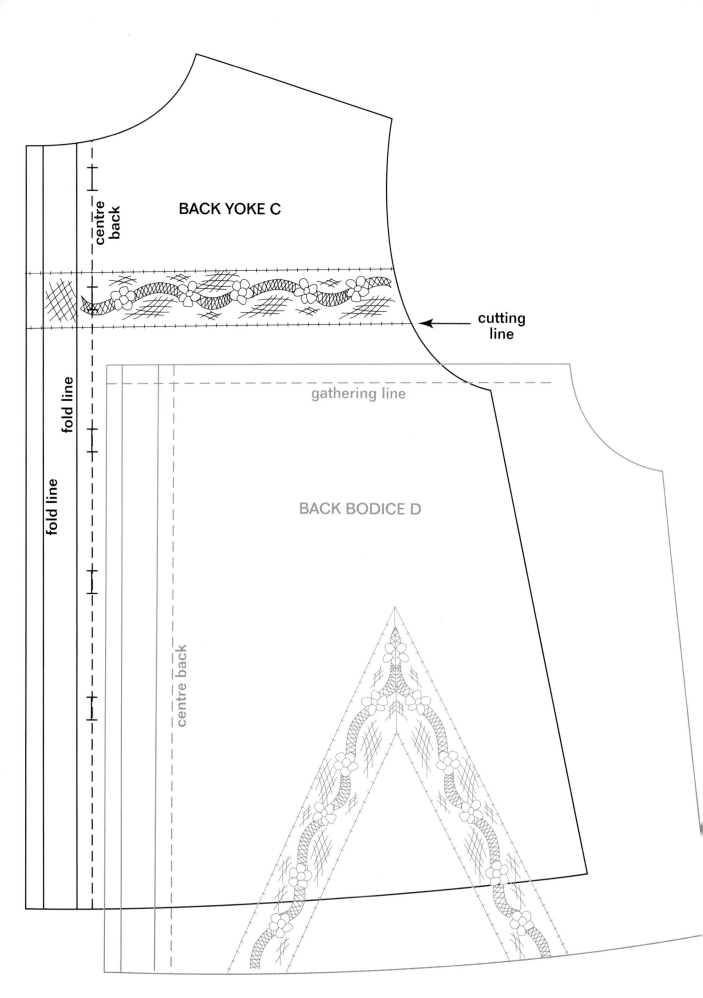

BACK YOKE C

centre back

cutting line

fold line

fold line

fold line

gathering line

BACK BODICE D

centre back

PANSY

By Barbara Willis

Where else would you find a cheeky doll named
Pansy but resting on a bed of foliage and flowers?
In fact, she looks a little like a flower herself.

The face can be painted before or after the doll is assembled. If you do it before, you will be able to paint on both the front and back, then choose the one you like the best.

SIZE

Finished size: 33 cm (13 in)

MATERIALS

23 cm (9 in) of flesh-coloured fabric for the body
23 cm (9 in) of pansy print fabric
23 cm (9 in) of purple fabric
23 cm (9 in) of yellow fabric
60 cm (24 in) of 12 mm ($^1/_2$ in) wide silk or taffeta ribbon
Sakura Micro Pigma fabric pens: Brown, Black, Pink or Red
Acrylic paints: White, Green, Black, Lavender
Coloured pencils: Pink, Green
Small paintbrush

Small quantity of hair fibre
Polyester fibre fill
Tracing paper
Pencil
Sewing thread
Craft glue

BEFORE YOU BEGIN

See the patterns on page 25. All seams are 6 mm ($^1/_4$ in). Read all the instructions and the section on making cloth dolls on page 12.

CONSTRUCTION

FOR THE BODY

STEP ONE

Trace all the pattern pieces. Trace the arm and leg pieces twice. Cut a piece 45.7 cm x 12.75 cm (18 in x 5 in) from the flesh-coloured fabric and from the purple fabric. Join them along one long side (Fig. 1).

STEP TWO

Fold the joined piece of fabric over double, lengthwise, with the right sides together. Pin the pattern pieces for the body and arms on the fabric as shown in figure 2.

STEP THREE

Stitch around the body and arms, leaving the bottom edges of all the pieces open. Cut out the body and two arms, leaving a 6 mm ($^1/_4$ in) seam allowance all around. Trim the seam allowance around the fingers back to 3 mm ($^1/_8$ in). Clip into the seam allowance between the thumb and forefinger.

STEP FOUR

Stitch the small dart in the front and back body pieces. Turn all the pieces to the right side.

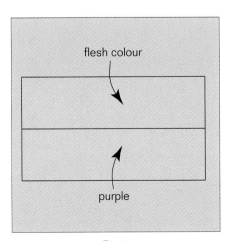

flesh colour

purple

Fig. 1

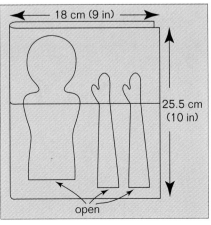

18 cm (9 in)

25.5 cm (10 in)

open

Fig. 2

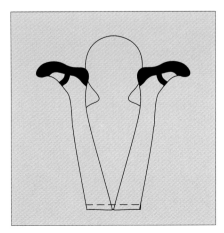

Fig. 3

STEP FIVE

Fold the remaining flesh-coloured fabric over double, with the right sides together. Pin both leg pattern pieces onto the fabric. Stitch around them, leaving the top edges open. Cut out the legs, leaving a 6 mm ($^1/_4$ in) seam allowance all around. Turn the legs to the right side. Stuff the legs firmly, up to 12 mm ($^1/_2$ in) from the top.

STEP SIX

Using the lavender acrylic paint, paint on the shoes. When the paint is quite dry, attach the legs to the front part of the body only (Fig. 3).

STEP SEVEN

Stuff the head and body firmly. Hand-sew the bottom edge of the body closed. Stuff the arms up to the elbows. Tie off at the elbows by winding thread around, then continue stuffing up to 12 mm ($^1/_2$ in) from the top. Sew the arms securely to the body at the points marked, taking care that both the arms face in the correct direction.

FOR THE FACE

STEP ONE

With the lead pencil, lightly draw in two circles for the irises. Paint in the circles with the Green acrylic paint (Fig. 4).

STEP TWO

Using the Black Pigma pen, draw in the upper eyelids. Shade and enhance the eyelids with the Brown Pigma pen.

STEP THREE

Using the Black Pigma pen, draw in the eyelashes and the eyebrows. Paint in the pupil with either the Black pen or Black paint. With the White acrylic paint, add a highlight to each eye.

STEP FOUR

Draw in the nose with the Brown Pigma pen and the mouth with the Pink or the Red Pigma pen.

STEP FIVE

To complete the face, add some blusher to the cheeks, using the Pink coloured pencil, and with the Green coloured pencil, add some shadow to the upper eyelid.

FOR THE COSTUME

STEP ONE

Trace the skirt petal from the pattern sheet. Using the tracing as your pattern, draw six petals onto the wrong side of the yellow fabric.

STEP TWO

Pin the yellow fabric to the pansy fabric, with the right sides facing. Stitch around the six petals, leaving the top edges open. Cut out the six petals, leaving a 6 mm ($^1/_4$ in) seam allowance all around. Turn the petals to the right side and press. Turn down 12 mm ($^1/_2$ in) at the top of each petal and stitch it to form a casing. Thread the ribbon through the casings of all six petals. Tie the petal skirt around the doll's waist, finishing with a pretty bow.

STEP THREE

Cut two rectangles of pansy fabric, each 25.5 cm x 9 cm (10 in x $3^1/_2$ in). With the right sides facing, stitch the short ends together to form a loop. Turn the loop to the right side. Using doubled sewing thread, hand-sew a line of running stitches 6 mm ($^1/_4$ in) from the raw edges (Fig. 5). Pull up the threads to gather the piece around the doll's arm, turning the raw edges to the inside. Knot the threads securely. Using 12 cm ($4^3/_4$ in) of ribbon, tie a small bow around each wrist.

STEP FOUR

Hand-sew a line of running stitches along the centre of a 30.5 cm (12 in) length of ribbon. Pull up the gathering so that the ribbon fits across the bodice front. Tie off the threads and hand-sew the ribbon into place.

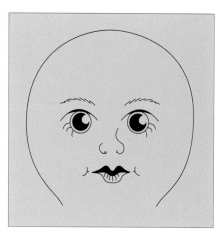

Fig. 4

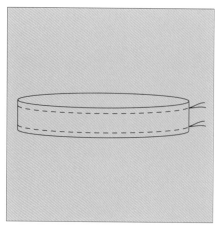

Fig. 5

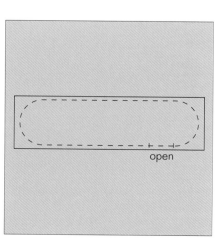

open

Fig. 6

STEP FIVE

Glue on a small quantity of hair fibre for the fringe (bangs). To make the hat, cut two 10 cm x 43 cm (4 in x 17 in) rectangles, one from the purple fabric and one from the yellow fabric. Place the two rectangles together, with the right sides facing. Stitch around the outside, rounding off the short edges and leaving a small opening for turning as shown (Fig. 6). Trim the seam at the ends to 6 mm ($^{1}/_{4}$ in). Turn the hat to the right side and press.

STEP SIX

With doubled sewing thread, sew two rows of running stitches as shown in figure 7. Pull up the back gathering tightly and tie off the threads to secure. Pull up the front gathering to fit around the doll's face and secure the threads. Baste the hat to the doll's head.

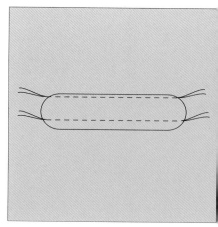

Fig. 7

The face is completed in a combination of pens for the fine drawing and paints for the shading

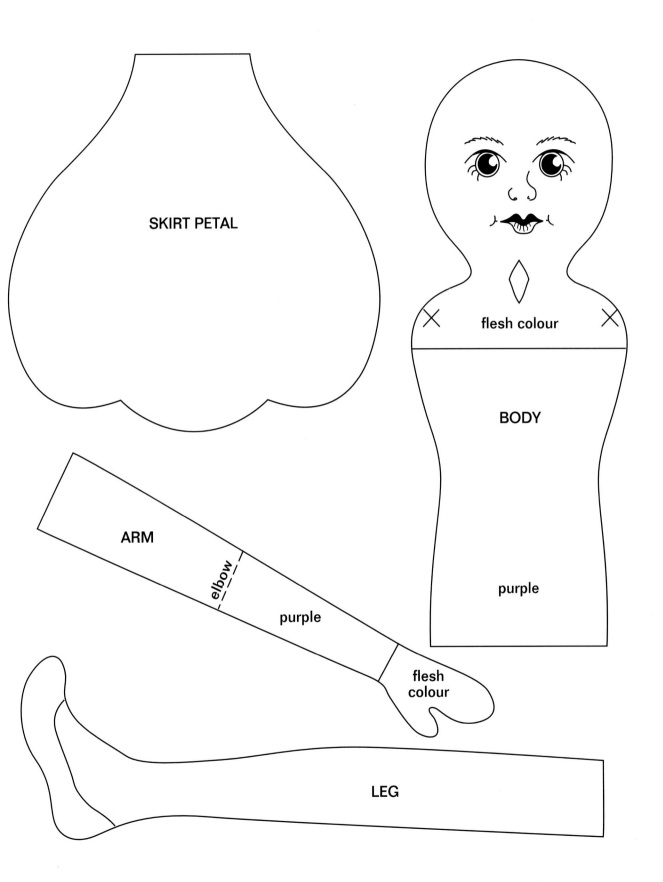

SKIRT PETAL

flesh colour

BODY

ARM

elbow

purple

purple

flesh
colour

LEG

SWEET PEA

By Anne's Glory Box

Sweet Pea has her own travelling wardrobe. In the photograph,
she is wearing a dress made from an embroidered handkerchief,
while her party dress hangs in the wardrobe.

SIZE

To fit a 23 cm (9 in) doll

MATERIALS

For the handkerchief dress
30 cm (12 in) square embroidered
  handkerchief
10 cm (4 in) of princess tape
Three small buttons
Matching sewing thread
For the petticoat
20 cm (8 in) of cotton voile
1 m (1¹⁄₈ yd) of 1 cm (³⁄₈ in) wide
  lace edging
One small button
Embroidery thread
For the party dress
25.5 cm x 30.5 cm (10 in x 12 in)
  of cotton voile
1 m (1¹⁄₈ yd) of 1 cm (³⁄₈ in) wide
  lace edging
4 m (4¹⁄₂ yd) of 26 mm (1¹⁄₈ in) wide
  lace edging
35 cm (14 in) of beading
Narrow ribbon
Pintucking foot for the sewing
  machine
Twin needle
Matching sewing thread
Press studs

BEFORE YOU BEGIN

See the patterns on page 28. All the
seams are 6 mm (¹⁄₄ in). Read all the
instructions and the section on dressing dolls, beginning on page 6.

HANDKERCHIEF DRESS

STEP ONE

Following the cutting layout diagram in
figure 1, cut out the parts of the dress.
Gather the raw long edge of the front
and back skirt frills to fit the bottom
edges of the front and back dress. With
the right sides together and the raw
edges even, attach the frills with small
hand or machine stitches.

STEP TWO

Neaten the centre back edges of the
dress by turning in a tiny hem on both
sides.

STEP THREE

Gather the raw long edge of the sleeve
frills to fit the bottom edges of the
sleeves. Attach the sleeve frills in the
same way as for the dress frills.

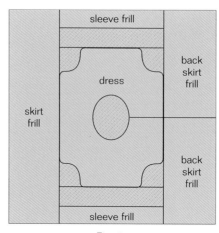

Fig. 1

STEP FOUR

With the right sides together, join th
side and underarm seams in one con
tinuous seam.

STEP FIVE

Sew the princess tape around the nec
edge, turning under the raw ends.

STEP SIX

Sew three small buttonhole stitc
loops on one side of the back openin
and sew on three small buttons t
correspond.

PETTICOAT

STEP ONE

Using the pattern provided, cut ou
a front and a back petticoat. On th
back petticoat, slash down the centr
back for 5 cm (2 in). Cut a strip of voil
2.5 cm x 12.7 cm (1 in x 5 in). Press
over double, lengthwise. With the raw
edges matching, stitch the strip aroun
both sides of the slash with a 6 mn
(¹⁄₄ in) seam, pivoting at the botton
point. Turn the strip to the inside an
slipstitch it over the seam.

STEP TWO

Join the shoulder seams, then neate
the raw edges with a small zigza
stitch. Sew lace edging around th
neck and the armhole edges. Sew th
side seams, then attach lace to th
bottom edge.

STEP THREE

Embroider the petticoat in feather stitch as shown on the pattern. Sew a buttonhole-stitch loop on one side of the opening and a small button on the other side to correspond.

PARTY DRESS

STEP ONE

Stitch twenty-seven rows of pintucking down the 25 cm (10 in) length of the fabric, beginning in the centre of the fabric and placing the pintucks 3 mm ($^1/_8$ in) apart. The pintucking should cover an area approximately 12 cm ($4^3/_4$ in) wide.

STEP TWO

Using the pattern provided, cut out the bodice from the pintucked fabric.

STEP THREE

Cut five 61 cm (24 in) lengths of the 26 mm ($1^1/_8$ in) wide lace edging for the skirt. Stitch the pieces one onto the other to form a panel, then cut the panel into two 30.5 cm (12 in) lengths. Cut one of the pieces in half to form two 15.25 cm (6 in) lengths for the backs. Gather the front and back skirts to fit the bottom edges of the bodice. Attach the skirt with a small seam, then neaten the seam with a small zigzag stitch.

STEP FOUR

Stitch two layers of the 1 cm ($^3/_8$ in) wide lace edging to the sleeve ends to form cuffs, then stitch the 1 cm ($^3/_8$ lace edging around the neck edge.

STEP FIVE

Join the side and underarm seams one continuous seam.

STEP SIX

Fold a length of 1 cm ($^3/_8$ in) lace ed ing over double and slipstitch it ov the centre back opening edges.

STEP SEVEN

Stitch the beading over the sea where the lace skirt joins the bodic turning under the raw edges at th centre back. Thread the ribb through the beading. Sew press stu along the back opening.

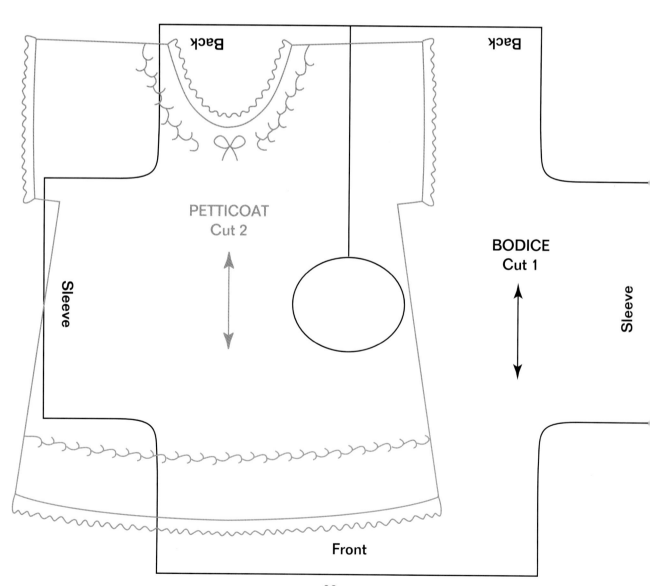

BABY EMMA

By Colleen Potts

A christening is such a special occasion that a special
dress is an absolute must. Emma's beautiful dress and
lace bonnet are just perfect.

SIZE

fit a 46 cm (18 in) baby doll

MATERIALS

) cm (24 in) of cotton lawn for the
petticoat
5 cm (34 in) of Swiss Nelona for the
dress and the bonnet
m (6¹/₂ yd) of 4 mm (³/₁₆ in) wide
silk ribbon
m (1¹/₈ yd) of 3.5 cm (1³/₈ in) wide
insertion lace
6 m (4 yd) of 1.5 cm (⁵/₈ in) wide
insertion lace
3 m (3⁵/₈ yd) of 4 cm (1¹/₂ in) lace
edging
5 m (2³/₄ yd) of 1.5 cm (⁵/₈ in) wide
lace edging
m (2¹/₄ yd) of 1 cm (³/₈ in) wide
beading
hirring elastic
ress studs or small buttons
intucking foot for the sewing
machine
win needle
latching sewing thread

BEFORE YOU BEGIN

ee the patterns on pages 32-33. All
eams are 6 mm (¹/₄ in). Read all the
istructions and the section on dress-
ig dolls beginning on page 6.

CUTTING

For the petticoat: Cut a 46 cm (18 in)
long piece across the full width of
the dress fabric for the petticoat skirt.
Cut two front and four back bodices.
For the skirt: Cut a 36 cm (14 in) long
piece across the full width of the dress
fabric.
For the front panel: Cut a piece 32 cm
x 36 cm (12¹/₂ in x 14 in).
For the frills: Cut two 8 cm (3¹/₈ in)
wide strips across the full width of the
dress fabric.
For the sleeves: Cut two pieces of
fabric, each 20 cm x 22 cm (7⁷/₈ in x
8⁵/₈ in). Zigzag the 1.5 cm (⁵/₈ in) wide
insertion lace down the centre of each
piece. Sew three pintucks, 1 cm (³/₈ in)
apart, on either side of the lace. Carefully, cut away the fabric from under
the insertion lace. Place the two pieces
together with the right sides facing,
then cut out two sleeves.
For the bodice: Cut two bodice fronts
and four bodice backs. You can create
the outer front bodice in any style you
wish: pintucked, pieced lace or a combination of both. If you choose pintucking and lace, cut a piece of fabric
12 cm x 24 cm (4³/₄ in x 9¹/₂ in), sew the
pintucks and lace, press, then cut out
the outer front bodice. If you choose
lace alone, zigzag the insertion lace,
beading and lace edging together to
create a piece that is 12 cm x 24 cm
(4³/₄ in x 9¹/₂ in). Thread ribbon through
the beading. Cut the outer front bodice
from the created piece.

DRESS

BODICE

STEP ONE

With the right sides facing, join the
shoulder seams of the bodice and of
the bodice lining.

STEP TWO

Place the bodice and lining together,
with the right sides facing. Stitch along
the back opening edges and around
the neckline. Trim the seam, clipping
into the curves, then turn the bodice to
the right side. Press carefully.

STEP THREE

Gently gather a length of 1.5 cm (⁵/₈ in)
wide lace edging to fit around the neck
edge. Slipstitch the lace into place.

STEP FOUR

Join the side seams of the bodice and of
the lining with French seams. Press.
From here on, treat the bodice as a
single piece.

FOR THE SLEEVES

STEP ONE

Zigzag a length of the 1.5 cm (⁵/₈ in)
wide lace edging to the sleeve ends.
Sew two rows of shirring elastic on

each sleeve, placing the first row 1 cm (³/₈ in) from the lace.

STEP TWO

With the right sides facing, sew each sleeve seam, using a small French seam.

STEP THREE

Gather the sleeve heads with two rows of small running stitches. Pull up the gathering to fit the armholes, then sew the sleeves into the armholes. Zigzag over the raw edges to neaten the seam.

FOR THE SKIRT

STEP ONE

On the front panel, sew pintucks 1 cm (³/₈ in) apart, parallel to the 36 cm (14 in) side. Zigzag the two widths of insertion lace in a V shape over the pintucking as marked on the pattern. (You could use beading for this step, if you prefer.) Carefully, cut away the pintucked fabric from behind the lace.

STEP TWO

On the skirt piece, beginning 3 cm (1¹/₄ in) from the bottom edge, sew four rows of pintucks, 1 cm (³/₈ in) apart.

STEP THREE

Cut two 36 cm (14 in) lengths of the 3.5 cm (1³/₈ in) wide insertion lace. Cut four 36 cm (14 in) lengths of beading. Zigzag a length of beading to both sides of each piece of insertion lace. Zigzag one of these joined lace pieces to either side of the pintucked lace panel.

STEP FOUR

Zigzag the skirt to the beading on either side of the front panel. Zigzag a length of the 1.5 cm (⁵/₈ in) wide insertion lace around the bottom edge of the skirt.

STEP FIVE

Mark the centre back of the skirt. Slash an 8 cm (3¹/₈ in) opening at the centre back. Bind the edges of this opening with a small piece of bias fabric.

STEP SIX

Join the frill pieces with a small French seam. Zigzag a length of the 4 cm (1¹/₂ in) wide lace edging to one long side of the frill. Gather the other long side of the frill to fit the bottom edge of the skirt, then zigzag the frill to the insertion lace on the bottom of the skirt.

TO COMPLETE

STEP ONE

Gather the top edge of the skirt to fit the bottom edge of the bodice. With the right sides facing, sew the skirt to the outer bodice, matching centre back and front. Turn under the seam allowance of the inner bodice, then slipstitch it over the seam.

STEP TWO

On the back opening, make small button loops and sew on the buttons to correspond or sew on press studs.

The bonnet features pieced and gathered lace

STEP THREE

Thread ribbon through the beading the skirt. Stitch a 36 cm (14 in) length ribbon to each wrist to tie a bow. Sti a small bow on the front bodice.

PETTICOAT

STEP ONE

With the right sides facing, join th shoulder seams of the bodice and the bodice lining. Place the bodice a lining together with the right sides fa ing. Stitch around the back openin neck and armhole edges. Trim and c the seams. Turn the bodice to the rig side and press.

STEP TWO

Open out the bodice at the underar edges. In one seam, join the sic seams of the bodice and of the linin Press.

STEP THREE

Zigzag a length of the 1.5 cm (⁵/₈ i insertion lace around the bottom of th skirt. Zigzag a length of the 1.5 c (⁵/₈ in) wide lace edging to the insertic lace.

STEP FOUR

Sew the skirt centre back seam, leav ing 8 cm (3¹/₈ in) open at the top edg Bind the edges of this opening as fc the dress or sew a narrow hem.

STEP FIVE

Gather the top edge of the skirt to fit th bodice. With the right sides facing, se the skirt to the outer bodice, matchin centre backs. Turn under the sear allowance on the bottom of the inne bodice, then slipstitch it over the sear

STEP SIX

Sew on button loops and buttons o press studs as for the dress.

BONNET

STEP ONE

Cut a piece of fabric 7 cm x 26 cm ($2^3/_4$ in x $10^1/_4$ in). On one 26 cm ($10^1/_4$ in) side, stitch a small casing.

STEP TWO

On the other 26 cm ($10^1/_4$ in) side, zigzag two rows of 1.5 cm ($^5/_8$ in) wide insertion lace, a row of beading and a row of 1.5 cm ($^5/_8$ in) wide lace edging. Make narrow hems on the two side raw edges, including the lace.

STEP THREE

Gather two 50 cm ($19^5/_8$ in) lengths of the 3.5 cm ($1^3/_8$ in) wide insertion lace. Zigzag one length of gathered lace to either side of the beading already in place.

STEP FOUR

Thread a length of ribbon through the casing. Pull the ribbon up firmly and tie the ends in a bow. Stitch a length of ribbon to either side of the bonnet front

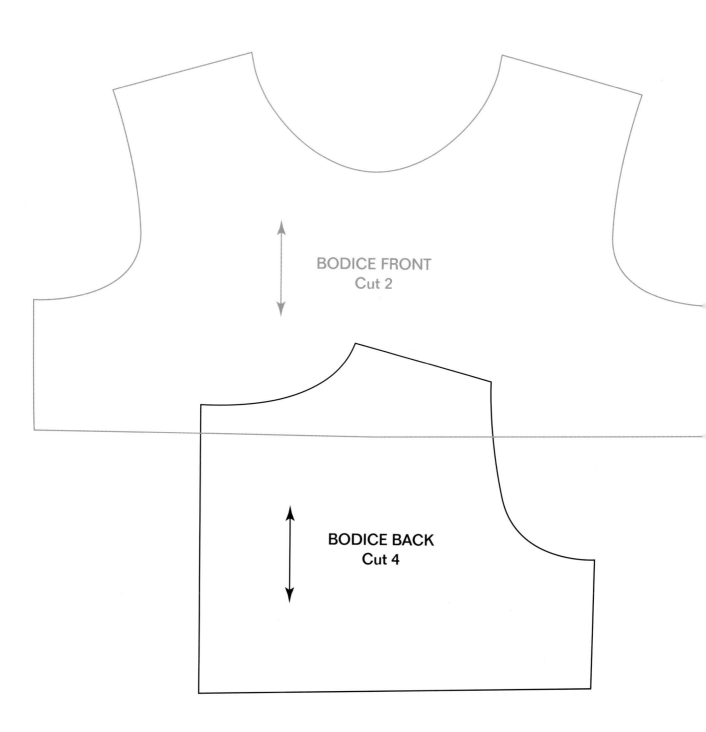

BODICE FRONT
Cut 2

BODICE BACK
Cut 4

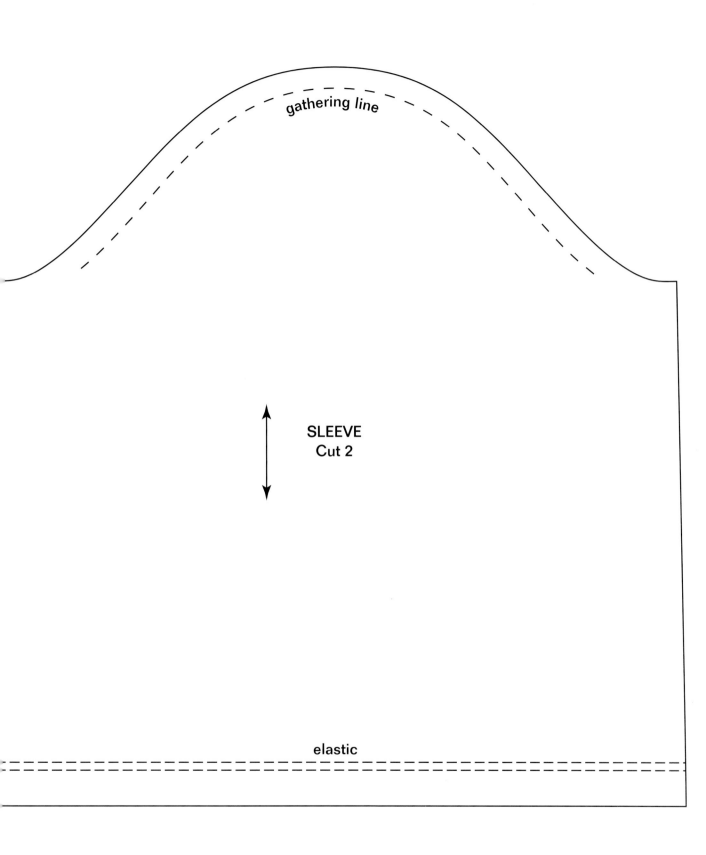

gathering line

SLEEVE
Cut 2

elastic

HEIDI

By Anne's Glory Box

Shimmering crushed velvet with a crisp white collar is Heidi's wardrobe choice for a day playing indoors with her teddy bear.

C rushed velvet contrasts beautifully with the crisp piqué, but you could choose any luxurious fabric.

SIZE

To fit a 49 cm (19 in) doll

MATERIALS

35 cm (14 in) of crushed velvet
20 cm (8 in) of piqué or cotton fabric for the collar and collar lining
1 m (1⅛ yd) of mini piping in a contrasting colour for the collar
2 m (2¼ yd) of 2.5 cm (1 in) wide white cotton lace edging
2.5 m (2¾ yd) of 6 mm (¼ in) wide lace edging in a contrasting colour
25 cm (10 in) of braid
Small floral brooch
Two press studs
6.5 cm (2½ in) of matching bias binding
Narrow elastic
Water-soluble pen or pencil
Tissue or tracing paper
Pencil
Fineline permanent marker pen
Matching sewing thread
Small sharp scissors

BEFORE YOU BEGIN

See the patterns on pages 36-37. All the seams are 6 mm (¼ in). Read all the instructions and the section on dressing dolls beginning on page 6. Trace the pattern onto tissue or tracing paper, using the marker pen.

CONSTRUCTION

FOR THE COLLAR

STEP ONE

Using the pattern provided, cut out the pattern pieces as instructed. On the right side of the collar, attach piping around the outer edge. Cut 122 cm (48 in) of the white lace edging and gather it to fit around the collar. Sew on the lace, using the zipper foot on your machine so you can stitch close to the piping.

STEP TWO

Fold the lace into the collar and pin it in place. With the right sides together, stitch the collar and the collar lining together around the outer edge, using the zipper foot as before and stitching over previous stitching rows.

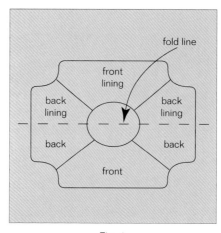

Fig. 1

STEP THREE

Turn the collar to the right side and press. Staystitch the neck edge.

FOR THE BODICE

STEP ONE

Using the pattern provided, cut out the pattern pieces as directed. Join the shoulder seams of the front and back bodices and linings so that you make a full circle of the bodice (Fig. 1).

STEP TWO

Pin the collar in place on the bodice from back fold to back fold. Fold the back linings and front lining over, so that the right sides are together. Stitch the neck edge. Snip across the corners and carefully clip the curve. Turn to the right side.

STEP THREE

Cut 40 cm (16 in) of the contrasting 6 mm (¼ in) wide lace edging. Gather the lace to fit the neckline and attach it with a zigzag stitch. Sew braid over the stitching.

STEP FOUR

On the back skirt, cut down the centre to the mark for the back opening. Bind the edges of the opening with matching bias binding. Gather the skirt front and back to fit the bodices. With right sides together, stitch the skirts to the bodices.

FOR THE SLEEVES

STEP ONE

Using the pattern provided, cut out the pattern pieces as directed. Using a small zigzag stitch, attach a piece of white lace edging to the bottom edge of each sleeve. Cut two lengths of elastic to suit your doll's wrists. Using a normal size zigzag stitch, attach the elastic so that it meets each edge. This will automatically gather each sleeve.

STEP TWO

Gather the sleeve heads to fit the armholes. Pin the sleeve into the armholes, then stitch.

STEP THREE

Stitch the side and underarm seams in one go.

TO COMPLETE

STEP ONE

Cut a piece of crushed velvet for the frill, 5 cm x 152 cm (2 in x 60 in). Join the ends to form a loop. Neaten the seam with overlocking or zigzag stitching.

STEP TWO

Attach the narrow lace edging to one edge of the frill and gather the other edge to fit the bottom of the skirt. With the right sides together, attach the frill to the skirt.

STEP THREE

Neaten the edges of the opening in the skirt back by hand. Sew on the press studs. Attach the brooch at the front.

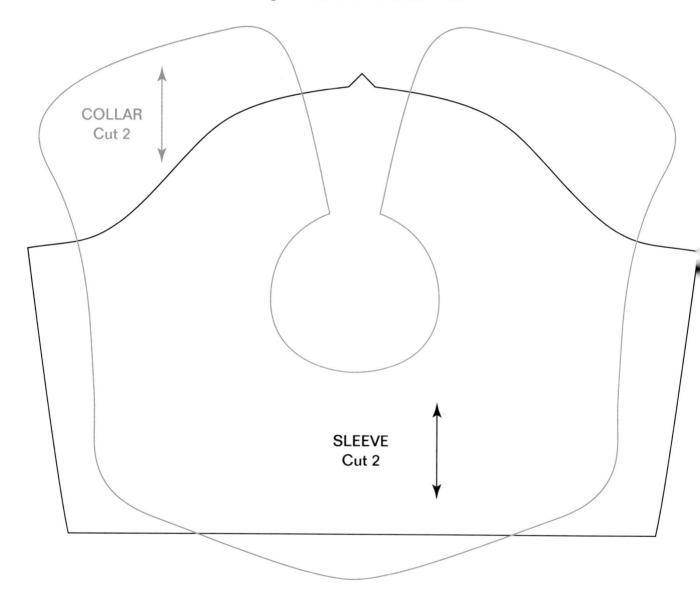

COLLAR
Cut 2

SLEEVE
Cut 2

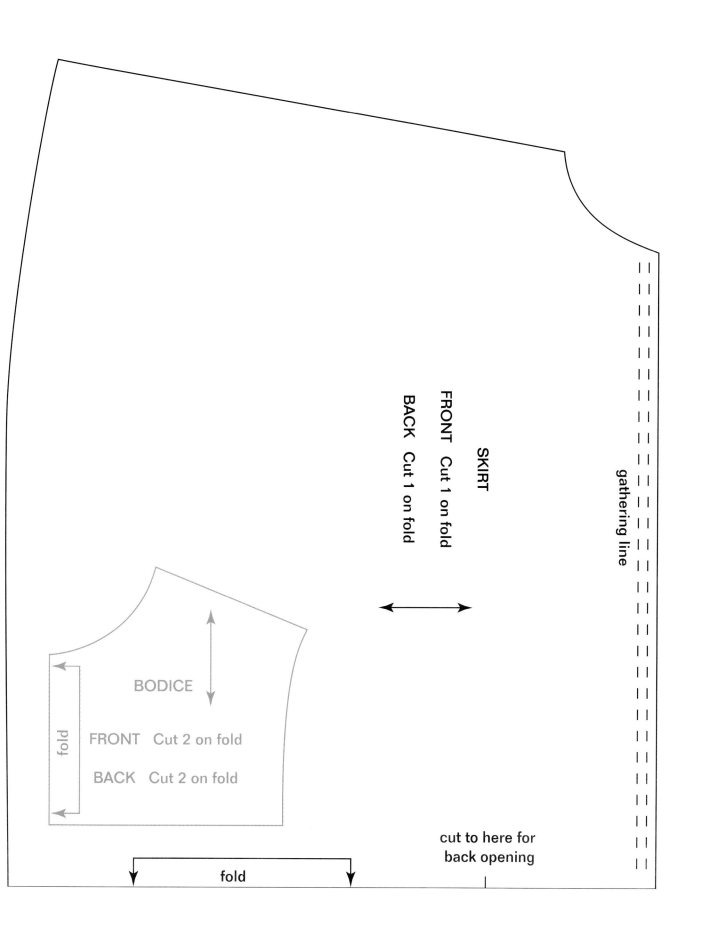

SKIRT

FRONT Cut 1 on fold

BACK Cut 1 on fold

gathering line

BODICE

FRONT Cut 2 on fold

BACK Cut 2 on fold

fold

fold

cut to here for
back opening

LILY

By Wendy Lee Ragan

**Resplendent in her best party dress
embroidered with bows and roses, Lily fills
in a creative moment as she awaits her beau.**

SIZE

To fit a 46 cm (18 in) doll

MATERIALS

50 cm (20 in) of cotton organza
25 cm (10 in) of fine tulle
1 m (1$^{1}/_{8}$ yd) of baby entredeux
35 cm (14 in) of 6 mm ($^{1}/_{4}$ in) wide
   entredeux
1 m (1$^{1}/_{8}$ yd) of 4 mm ($^{3}/_{16}$ in) wide
   silk ribbon
2 m (2$^{1}/_{4}$ yd) of 2 cm ($^{3}/_{4}$ in) wide
   lace edging
1 m (1$^{1}/_{8}$ yd) of 1.5 cm ($^{5}/_{8}$ in) wide
   lace edging
1.5 m (1$^{2}/_{3}$ yd) of 4 cm (1$^{1}/_{2}$ in) wide
   lace edging
DMC Stranded Cotton: Pink,
   Pale Pink, Blue, Pale Blue,
   Pale Yellow/Green
Crewel needles, size 8
Four or five small buttons
Embroidery hoop
Matching sewing thread
Water-soluble pen or pencil
Tracing paper
Press studs

BEFORE YOU BEGIN

See the patterns on pages 41-42. All
seams are 6 mm ($^{1}/_{4}$ in). Read all the
instructions and the section on dressing dolls beginning on page 6.

EMBROIDERY

STEP ONE

Cut two 20 cm (8 in) squares of
organza. Using the water-soluble pen
or pencil, trace the collar pattern and
embroidery design onto one piece
and the bodice pattern and embroidery design onto the other piece.

STEP TWO

Secure the organza in the embroidery
hoop, then embroider the designs in
the following order and stitches: first
work the straight lines in pale blue
back stitches, then the bows in shadow
embroidery and, finally, make the
bullion roses. (For tips on embroidery,
see pages 8-10.)

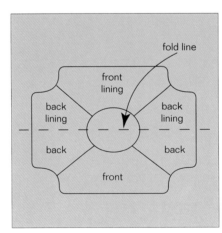

Fig. 1

CONSTRUCTION

FOR THE BODICE

STEP ONE

Using the patterns provided, cut out
one front bodice and collar from the
embroidered organza and one front
bodice and two back bodices (on the
fold) from the plain organza.

STEP TWO

Join the shoulder seams, joining the
front to the backs and the front lining to
the back linings, using a 3 mm ($^{1}/_{8}$ in)
seam (Fig. 1). Press all the seams open.
Fold the bodice and lining along the
fold line with the right sides facing.
Stitch around the neck edge.

STEP THREE

Join the side seams on the bodice and
on the bodice lining. Press the seams
open. Turn the bodice through to the
right side.

FOR THE SLEEVES

STEP ONE

Using the pattern provided, cut out the
pattern pieces as directed. Cut two
13 cm (5 in) lengths of the 6 mm ($^{1}/_{4}$ in)
wide entredeux. Using a normal stitch
length, gather the sleeve ends to fit the
entredeux. With the right sides facing,
stitch the entredeux to the sleeves.

Trim the seam and neaten with zigzag stitching.

STEP TWO

Trim the batiste from the other side of the entredeux. Cut two 25 cm (10 in) lengths of the 2 cm ($^3/_4$ in) wide lace edging. Gather the lace to fit the entredeux on the sleeve ends. Attach the lace edging with a small zigzag stitch.

STEP THREE

Using a normal stitch length, gather the sleeve heads to fit the armholes. Sew the seams into the armholes, then neaten the seams with zigzag stitching.

FOR THE SKIRT

STEP ONE

Cut a piece of organza, 15 cm x 61 cm (6 in x 24 in). Sew the centre back seam with a fine French seam up to 5 cm (2 in) from the top edge. Cut a strip of organza, 2 cm x 11.5 cm ($^3/_4$ in x 4$^1/_2$ in) and use it to bind the edges of the opening.

STEP TWO

Using a normal stitch length, gather the top edge of the skirt with three rows of stitching. Pull up the gathering to fit the bodice. Join the skirt to the bodice, leaving the bodice lining free. Turn under 3 mm ($^1/_8$ in) on the bottom edge of the bodice lining. Slipstitch the folded edge over the seam.

STEP THREE

Sew a length of the baby entredeux around the bottom edge of the skirt. Gather the 4 cm (1$^1/_2$ in) wide lace edging to fit the entredeux, then attach it with zigzag stitching.

FOR THE COLLAR

STEP ONE

Using the pattern provided, cut one collar from the embroidered organza and one from the plain organza. Place the two collar sections together with the right sides facing. Stitch around the outside edge. Trim and clip the seam allowance, then turn the collar through to the right side. Press.

STEP TWO

Turn under 3 mm ($^1/_8$ in) on both neck edges, clipping as necessary to ensure a smooth finish. Slipstitch the edge closed with tiny invisible stitches. Press.

STEP THREE

Hand-whip a length of trimmed baby entredeux around the outer edge of the collar. Gather 1 m (1$^1/_8$ yd) of the 1.5 cm ($^5/_8$ in) wide lace edging to fit around the collar. Hand-whip the lace edging to the entredeux.

STEP FOUR

Using very small slipstitches, sew the collar to the dress bodice around the neck edge, taking care to match centre fronts and centre backs.

TO COMPLETE

Make four or five small buttonholes by hand on the left back edge of the bodice. Sew on buttons to correspond.

PETTICOAT

STEP ONE

Cut two bodice fronts and two bodice backs, using the dress pattern. Make up the bodice as for the dress. Hand finish the armholes.

STEP TWO

Cut a piece of tulle 25 cm x 30 cm (10 in x 12 in). Fold the tulle so that it measures 15 cm x 25 cm (6 in x 10 in). Join the centre back seam, leaving a placket opening at the top. Gather the top edge of the tulle to fit the bodice and attach it in the same way as the skirt on the dress. Sew on press studs

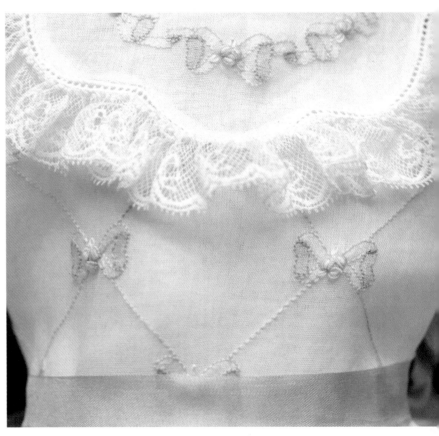

Beautiful embroidery is a feature of this dress

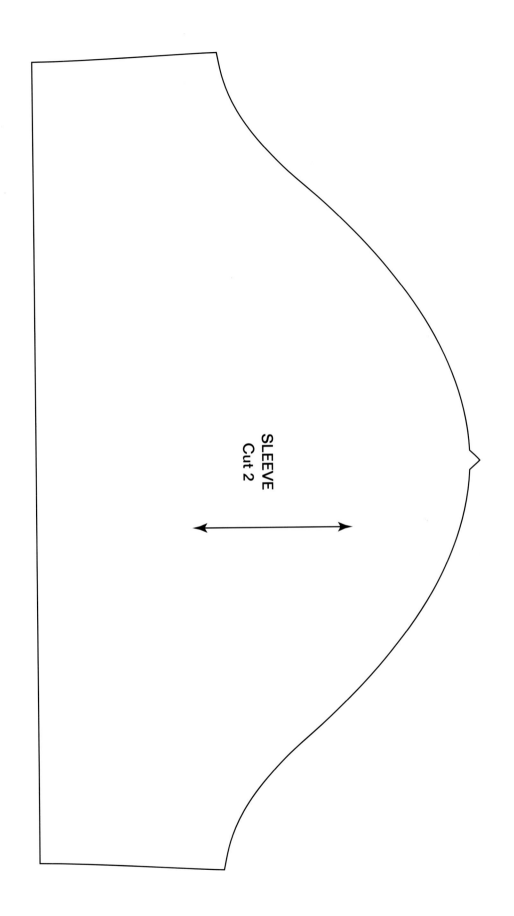

SLEEVE
Cut 2

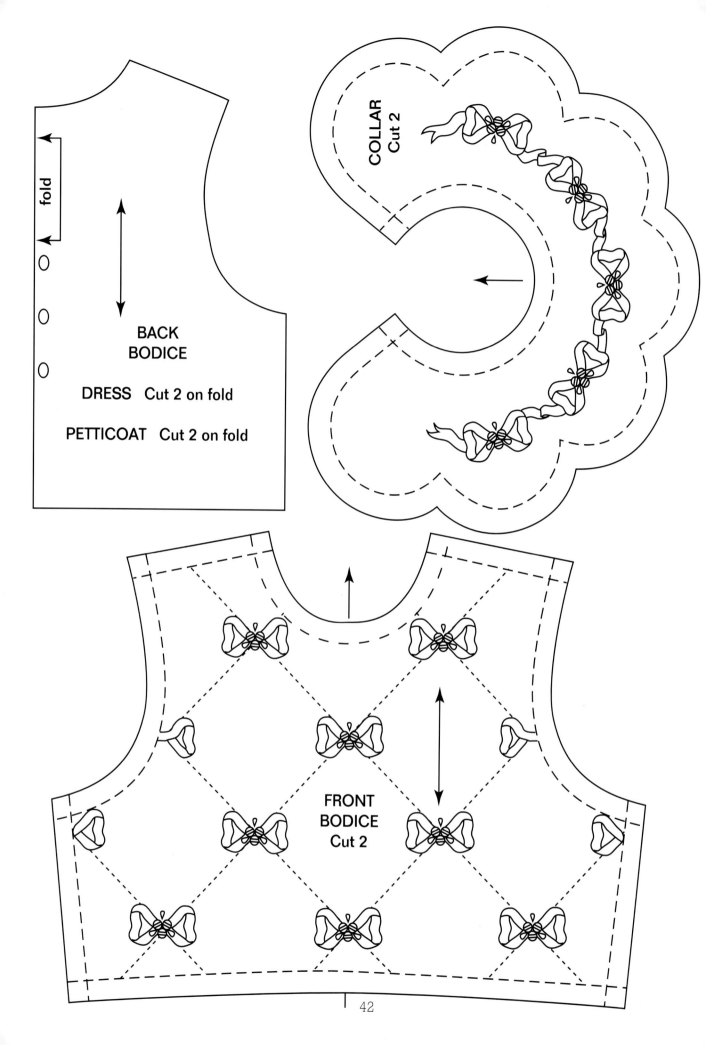

fold

BACK
BODICE

DRESS   Cut 2 on fold

PETTICOAT   Cut 2 on fold

COLLAR
Cut 2

FRONT
BODICE
Cut 2

42

LILLIBET

By Anne's Glory Box

A picture in peach, Lillibet is dressed for
a stroll in the park. One last glance in her
looking glass and she's off!

This lace-trimmed outfit includes a
half slip, camisole and knickers.

SIZE

o fit a 56-61 cm (22-24 in) doll

MATERIALS

m (1¹/₈ yd) of Swiss batiste
m (2¹/₄ yd) of 1.5 cm (⁵/₈ in) wide
lace edging
m (1¹/₈ yd) of 6 mm (¹/₄ in) wide
lace edging
m (4¹/₂ yd) of 12 mm (¹/₂ in) wide
insertion lace
3.6 m (4 yd) of beading
3.25 m (3¹/₂ yd) of entredeux
m (4¹/₂ yd) of 6 mm (¹/₄ in) wide
ribbon
Press studs
Narrow elastic

For the hat

Sinnamay hat
3.2 m (3¹/₂ yd) of 4.5 cm (1³/₄ in) wide
cotton lace edging
2 m (2¹/₄ yd) of 1 cm (³/₈ in) wide soft
grosgrain ribbon
1 m (1¹/₈ yd) of 12 mm (¹/₂ in) wide
green rayon ribbon

Note: If you can't buy lace edging with
this lovely soft look, you can achieve
the same result by tea dying white cotton lace. For instructions on tea dying
see page 7.

BEFORE YOU BEGIN

See the patterns on pages 48-49. All
seams are 6 mm (¹/₄ in). Read all the
instructions and the section on dressing dolls beginning on page 6.

HALF SLIP

STEP ONE

Cut a 61 cm (24 in) length of entredeux, beading, insertion lace (twice)
and the wider lace edging. Join the
laces together with a small zigzag
stitch in the order indicated in figure 1.

STEP TWO

Cut a piece of Swiss batiste 23 cm x
61 cm (9 in x 24 in). With the right sides
facing, join the fabric to the entredeux
on the lace piece. Using a small
straight stitch, stitch close to the edge
of the entredeux. Trim the seam to
3 mm (¹/₈ in), then neaten the edge with
a small zigzag stitch. Cut a 61 cm
(24 in) length of ribbon and thread it
through the beading on the lace.

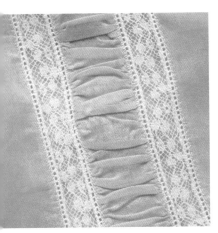

Unusual puffing detail on the bodice front

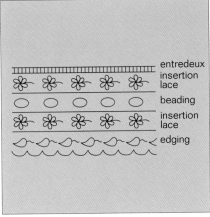

Fig. 1

(Figure labels: entredeux, insertion lace, beading, insertion lace, edging)

Panels of joined lace are a feature

STEP THREE

Join the centre back seam with a small French seam. Fold over 6 mm (¼ in) at the top edge, then fold over another scant 12 mm (½ in), forming a casing. Stitch, leaving a small opening for threading the elastic. Cut a length of elastic to fit the doll's waist snugly and insert the elastic into the casing. Secure the ends of the elastic and slipstitch the opening closed.

KNICKERS

STEP ONE

Using the pattern provided, cut out the knickers from the Swiss batiste as instructed on the pattern.

STEP TWO

Cut a 30.5 cm (12 in) length of entredeux, beading (twice), insertion lace (twice) and the wider lace edging. Join the laces together with a small zigzag stitch in the order indicated in figure 2.

STEP THREE

Attach the lace piece to the bottom edge of the knickers as for the half slip. Thread a 30.5 cm (12 in) length of ribbon through the row of beading closest to the fabric on each leg. Sew the leg seams with a small French seam.

STEP FOUR

Slip one leg inside the other so the wrong sides of both legs are facing. Sew the crotch seam with a small French seam.

STEP FIVE

Make a casing at the top edge in the same way as for the half slip. Thread ribbon through the remaining beading, leaving sufficiently long tails so that the ribbon can be used to gather up the legs to fit the doll, and tie into a bow.

CAMISOLE

STEP ONE

Cut 15 cm (6 in) lengths of entredeux (twice), beading (three times), and insertion lace (twice). Join the laces together with a small zigzag stitch as shown in figure 3.

STEP TWO

Cut two pieces of Swiss batiste, each 7.5 cm x 15 cm (3 in x 6 in). Attach one piece to the entredeux on the edges of the lace piece.

STEP THREE

Using the pattern provided and with the fabric folded so the beading on the lace piece is at the centre front, cut out the front camisole. Staystitch the neck and the bottom edges. Using the pattern provided, cut out the back camisole.

STEP FOUR

Join the shoulder and side seams with small French seams. Roll and whip the neck, arm and bottom edges. On the centre back edges, turn in 6 mm (¼ in) then another 12 mm (½ in) and stitch.

STEP FIVE

Attach a length of the wider lace edging at the bottom edge. Gently gather a length of the narrower lace edging and attach it to the neck and armhole edges with a small zigzag stitch. Sew press studs along the back opening.

DRESS

FOR THE SKIRT

STEP ONE

Cut 35.5 cm (14 in) lengths of entredeux (four times), insertion lace (four times), beading (twice). Join the laces with a small zigzag stitch as indicated in figure 4. Thread a length of lace through the beading on each piece.

STEP TWO

Cut two pieces of Swiss batiste, each 10 cm x 35.5 cm (4 in x 14 in). Measuring from the top, mark the sides for five pintucks as indicated in figure 5. Stitch the pintucks, then roll and whip the bottom edge of both pieces. Attach a length of 1.5 cm (⅝ in) wide lace edging to these edges.

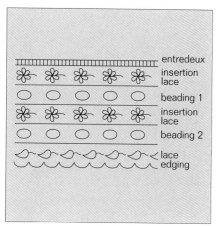

Fig. 2

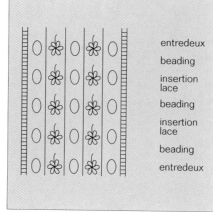

Fig. 3

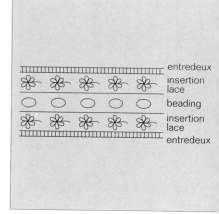

Fig. 4

Note: You can make pintucks using a twin needle and a pintucking foot on your sewing machine. First press each pleat, flatten the fabric, then stitch along the fold line. Alternatively, you can make the pintucks by folding and pressing on each marked line, then stitching 2 mm ($^1/_{16}$ in) from the pressed edge. Keep the pintucks straight and even, with each one the same width.

STEP THREE

Attach the top edge of each pintucked piece to the bottom edge of one joined lace piece, as before.

STEP FOUR

Cut two pieces of Swiss batiste, each 14 cm x 35.5 cm ($5^1/_2$ in x 14 in). Attach one piece of fabric to the entredeux on the top of each lace piece, as before.

STEP FIVE

At the centre back, cut down 7.5 cm (3 in) for the placket. Cut a strip of fabric, 2.5 cm x 15 cm (1 in x 6 in). With the right sides together, stitch the strip to the placket opening, starting with a seam allowance of 6 mm ($^1/_4$ in) at the top and tapering right down at the base. Pivot at the base, then stitch up the other side, widening the seam out to 6 mm ($^1/_4$ in) at the top. Fold the binding strip over double, turning under the raw edge. Slipstitch the binding to the wrong side. Press.

FOR THE BODICE

STEP ONE

Cut a strip of Swiss batiste 4 cm x 30 cm ($1^1/_2$ in x 12 in) for the puffing strip. Using a normal stitch length, sew two rows of gathering down each side of the strip. Pull up the gathering so the strip measures 15 cm (6 in) long. Even out the gathering. Roll and whip the edges.

STEP TWO

Cut 15 cm (6 in) lengths of entredeux (four times) and insertion lace (twice). Join the laces together to make two pieces, as shown in figure 6. Attach one

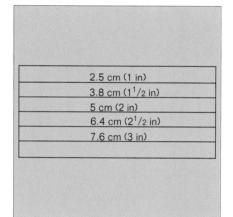

2.5 cm (1 in)
3.8 cm ($1^1/_2$ in)
5 cm (2 in)
6.4 cm ($2^1/_2$ in)
7.6 cm (3 in)

Fig. 5

joined lace piece to either side of t[
puffing piece as shown in figure 7.

STEP THREE

Cut two pieces of Swiss batiste, ea[
6.5 cm x 15 cm ($2^1/_2$ in x 6 in). Atta[
one piece of fabric to either side of t[
lace and puffing piece.

STEP FOUR

Using the pattern provided, cut t[
front bodice out of the fabric, lace a[
puffing piece, placing the centre of t[
puffing at the centre front. Staystitch t[
waist and the neck edges.

STEP FIVE

Cut out two back yokes from the Swi[
batiste. Neaten the centre back edg[
as for the camisole. Join the should[
seam with small French seams.

FOR THE SLEEVES

STEP ONE

Cut 20 cm (8 in) lengths of entrede[
(twice), insertion lace (four times[
beading (four times) and lace edgi[
(twice). Join the laces together to mal[
two pieces as shown in figure 8.

STEP TWO

Using the pattern provided, cut out tw[
sleeves from the Swiss batiste. Roll ar[

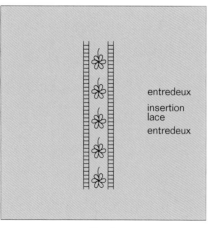

entredeux
insertion lace
entredeux

Fig. 6

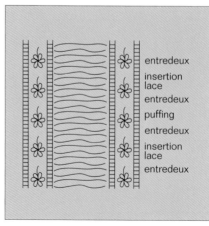

entredeux
insertion lace
entredeux
puffing
entredeux
insertion lace
entredeux

Fig. 7

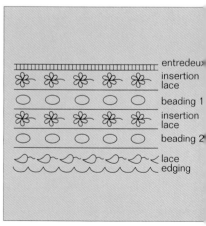

entredeu[
insertion lace
beading 1
insertion lace
beading 2
lace edging

Fig. 8

46

whip the bottom edges of the sleeves, then attach the joined lace pieces to these edges.

STEP THREE

Gather the sleeve heads to fit the armholes. Pin, then stitch the sleeves into the armholes. Trim the seam allowances to 3 mm ($^1/_8$ in), then neaten with zigzag stitching. Thread ribbon through the first row of beading.

TO COMPLETE

STEP ONE

Gather the top edge of the front and back skirts to fit the front and back bodice. Attach the skirts to the bodice sections. Neaten the seam with zigzag stitching.

STEP TWO

Sew the side and underarm seams with small French seams.

STEP THREE

Using straight stitches, sew a length of entredeux around the neck edge. Trim the seam allowance to 3 mm ($^1/_8$ in), then neaten the seam with zigzag stitching. Attach a length of insertion lace to the entredeux, then attach a gently gathered length of the 6 mm ($^1/_4$ in) wide lace edging to the insertion lace.

STEP FOUR

Stitch a length of beading around the waist, over the seam. Thread ribbon through the beading. Neaten the ends of the ribbon.

STEP FIVE

Sew press studs on the back opening edges. Thread ribbon through the second row of beading on the sleeves, pulling up the sleeves to fit the doll.

HAT

STEP ONE

Using a small flat seam, join the ends of a 70 cm (27$^1/_2$ in) length of lace edging. Gather the lace, then pin it under the hat brim. Adjust the gathering, then stitch it into place with a neat back stitch, placing the seam in the lace at the back and having the edge of the lace even with the edge of the hat brim.

STEP TWO

Join the ends of a 90 cm (35$^1/_2$ in) length of lace edging as before. Gather the lace and pin it to the brim. Stitch the lace into place, taking care not to stitch through the lace under the brim.

STEP THREE

Cut two 75 cm (29$^1/_2$ in) lengths of lace. Overlap the straight edges of the lace by at least 12 mm ($^1/_2$ in). Sew a row of gathering stitches along the centre of the overlap. Gather the lace to fit around the crown. Pin, then stitch the lace to the crown, stitching along the gathering line.

STEP FOUR

Using the grosgrain ribbon, make several ribbon roses, wrapping the base of each rose securely with thread. Using the green rayon ribbon, make three loops and attach them to the base of each rose by wrapping with thread. Stitch the roses and leaves to the hat along the line of the gathering

Camisole, half slip and knickers complete the set

47

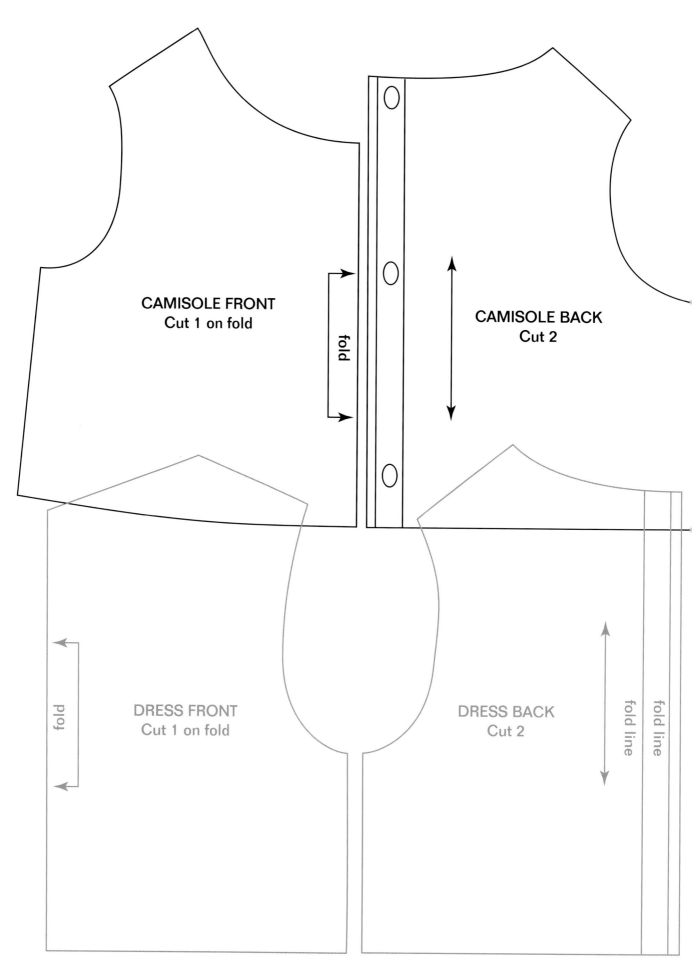

CAMISOLE FRONT
Cut 1 on fold

fold

CAMISOLE BACK
Cut 2

DRESS FRONT
Cut 1 on fold

fold

DRESS BACK
Cut 2

fold line

fold line

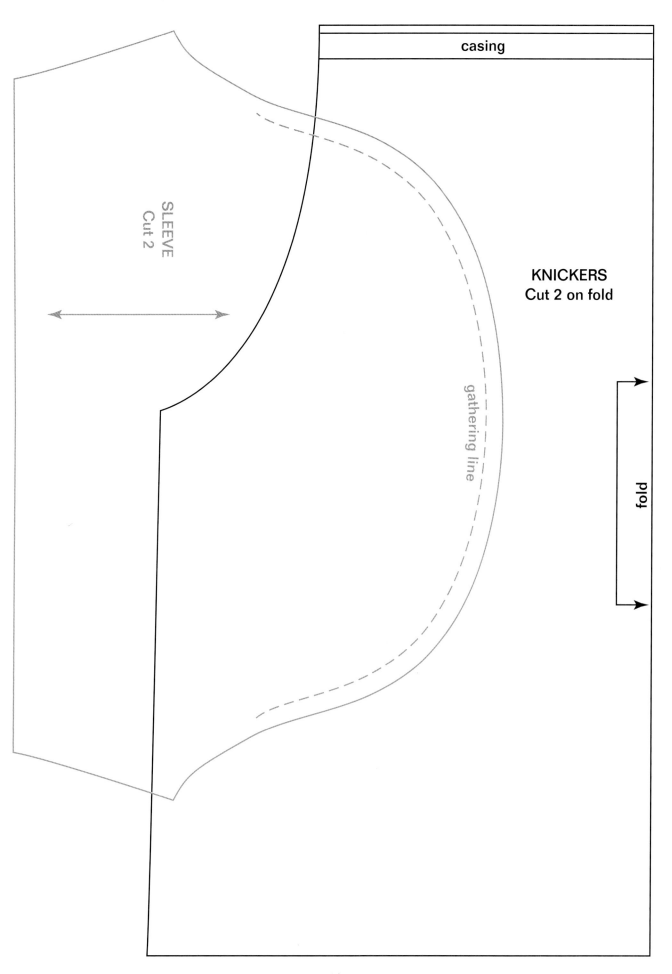

casing

SLEEVE
Cut 2

KNICKERS
Cut 2 on fold

gathering line

fold

49

REBECCA

By Piecemakers General Store

A country girl's work is never done – especially when there are pots to prepare for planting. Thank goodness she can sit down!

Wood stain and varnish have been used to create the appearance of a wooden doll.

SIZE

Finished size: 48 cm (19 in)

MATERIALS

40 cm (16 in) of fabric for the dress
50 cm (20 in) of fabric for the body
Polyester fibre fill
140 cm (54 in) of 12 mm ($\frac{1}{2}$ in) wide cotton lace
50 cm (20 in) of 6 mm ($\frac{1}{4}$ in) wide elastic
2 m (2$\frac{1}{4}$ yd) cotton curling for the hair
Crocheted table runner
Acrylic paints: Off-white, Blue, Brown, White, Pink
Small paintbrush for the features
2.5 cm (1 in) paintbrush
Sakura Micro Pigma fabric pen, Black
Wood stain, pine colour
Clear varnish, satin finish
Glue gun
One small button
Press studs

BEFORE YOU BEGIN

See the patterns on pages 53–55. All seams are 6 mm ($\frac{1}{4}$ in) unless stated otherwise. Read all the instructions and the section on making cloth dolls on page 12.

CONSTRUCTION

FOR THE BODY

STEP ONE

Using the patterns provided, cut out the body, body gussets, arms and legs as instructed on the pattern.

STEP TWO

With the right sides facing, join the front and back body between **A** and **B**. Beginning at the centre bottom, pin and stitch the side gussets in place, leaving the bottom seam of the gusset open. Turn the body through to the right side. Fill the body quite firmly; this doll has a fairly flat face.

STEP THREE

With the right sides facing, join the arms in pairs, taking care to make a

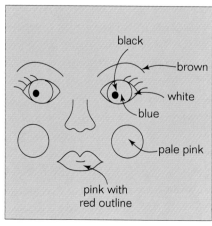

black
brown
white
blue
pale pink
pink with red outline

Fig. 1

right and a left arm. Turn the arms through to the right side. Fill the hands lightly so that you are still able to stitch the fingers. Stitch the fingers as marked. Fill quite firmly from the wrists to the elbow. Stitch across at the elbow. Fill lightly from the elbow to the shoulder, then stitch across the top of the arm to close it. Attach one arm firmly to each shoulder across the gusset, making sure both hands face the right way.

STEP FOUR

With the right sides facing, join the legs in pairs. Turn the legs through to the right side. Fill the legs firmly to the knees. Turn the leg so that the seam runs down the centre of the leg. Stitch across the leg at the knee. Lightly fill the leg to the top, stitching across to close the leg. Attach the legs to the body at the front so that the gusset makes a bottom.

STEP FIVE

With the white acrylic paint, paint the head, hands and legs. Allow the paint to dry, then add another coat. Paint the shoes and socks. Allow the paint to dry.

FOR THE FACE

Paint on the facial features as shown (Fig. 1). Brush the wood stain over the previous painting, carefully wiping off any excess. When the wood stain is thoroughly dry, brush on a coat of varnish.

FOR THE HAIR

To make the hair, cut the cotton curling into 7.5 cm (3 in) pieces. Using an awl or something similar, make small holes all over the head inside the hairline. Fold each length of hair over double and push the folded end into a hole. Glue into place securely. Take care to cover the head well so there are no unsightly gaps. When the glue is dry, tease the hair out.

DRESS

STEP ONE

Using the pattern provided, cut two front and four back bodices. Sew the shoulder and side seams of the bodice and the bodice lining.

STEP TWO

Place the bodice and bodice lining together with the right sides facing. Sew around the neck and the back opening edges. Trim and clip the seam allowances. Turn the bodice to the right side and press. Gather a length of lace edging and stitch it around the neckline.

STEP THREE

Cut two sleeves on the fold. Turn up and stitch a 12 mm ($^1/_2$ in) hem on the bottom of the sleeves to form a casing. Thread a length of elastic through the casing, catching the ends of the elastic at the fabric edges. Sew the sleeve seam, joining the ends of the elastic at the same time.

STEP FOUR

Gather the sleeve heads to fit the armholes. Pin and stitch the sleeves into the armholes. Neaten the seam allowances with zigzag stitching.

STEP FIVE

Cut a piece of fabric 30 cm x 85 cm ($11^3/_4$ in x $33^1/_2$ in) for the skirt. On one long side, turn up 6 mm ($^1/_4$ in), then turn up another 3.5 cm ($1^3/_8$ in) for the hem. Stitch and press. Sew a length of lace edging around the hem.

STEP SIX

Sew the centre back seam up to 2.5 cm (1 in) from the waist edge.

STEP SEVEN

Gather the other long side of the skirt to fit the bodice. With the right side facing, sew the skirt to the bodice. Neaten the seam allowances with zigzag stitching.

STEP EIGHT

Sew a buttonhole and button at the waist and press studs on the back opening edges.

PANTALOONS

From the crocheted table runner, cut two pantaloon pieces on the fold. Place the two pieces together and stitch from **A** to **B** on the front and on the back. Sew the crotch seam. Neaten the top edge with zigzag stitching, then turn over 12 mm ($^1/_2$ in) to make a casing. Stitch, leaving an opening for inserting the elastic. Insert the elastic and join the ends so that the waist fits snugly.

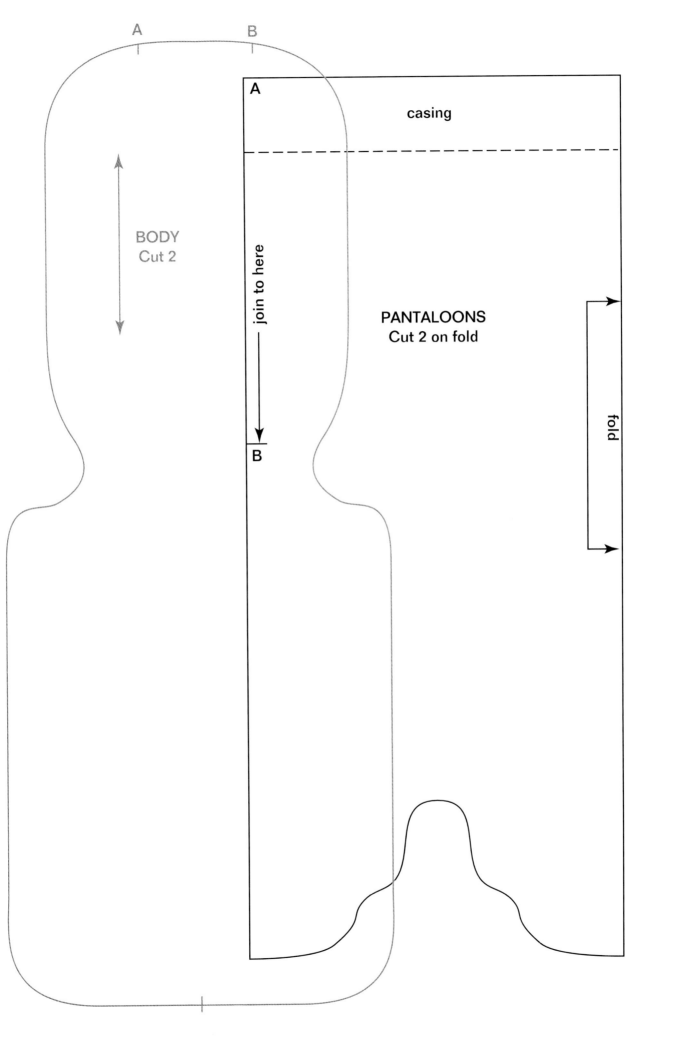

A

B

BODY
Cut 2

A

casing

join to here

B

PANTALOONS
Cut 2 on fold

fold

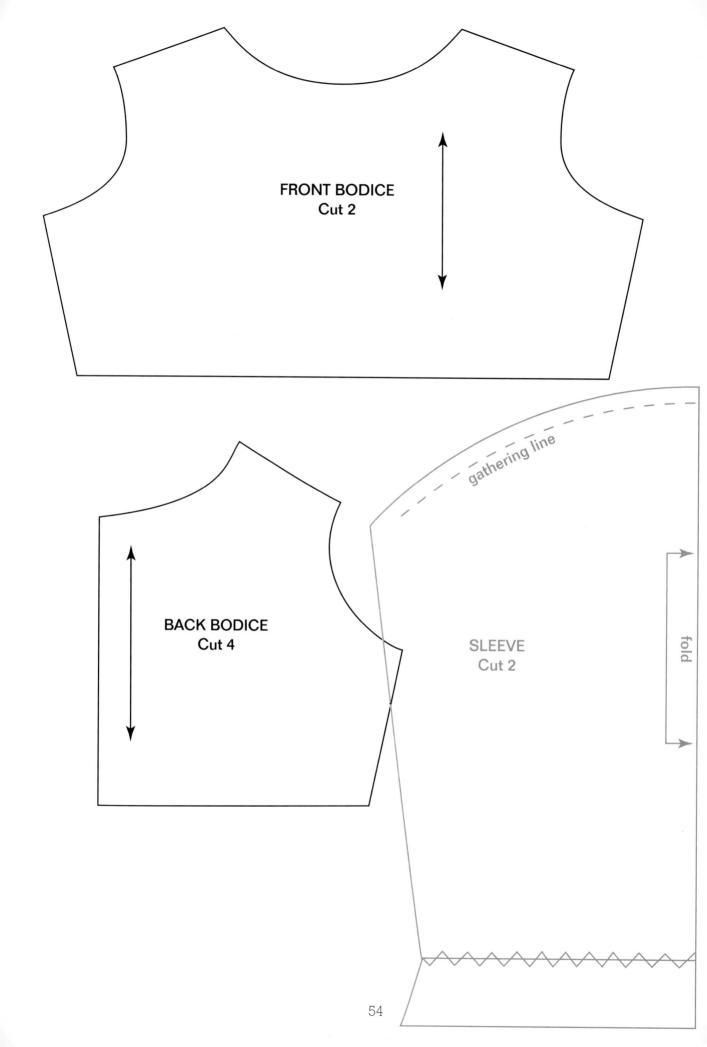

FRONT BODICE
Cut 2

BACK BODICE
Cut 4

SLEEVE
Cut 2

gathering line

fold

54

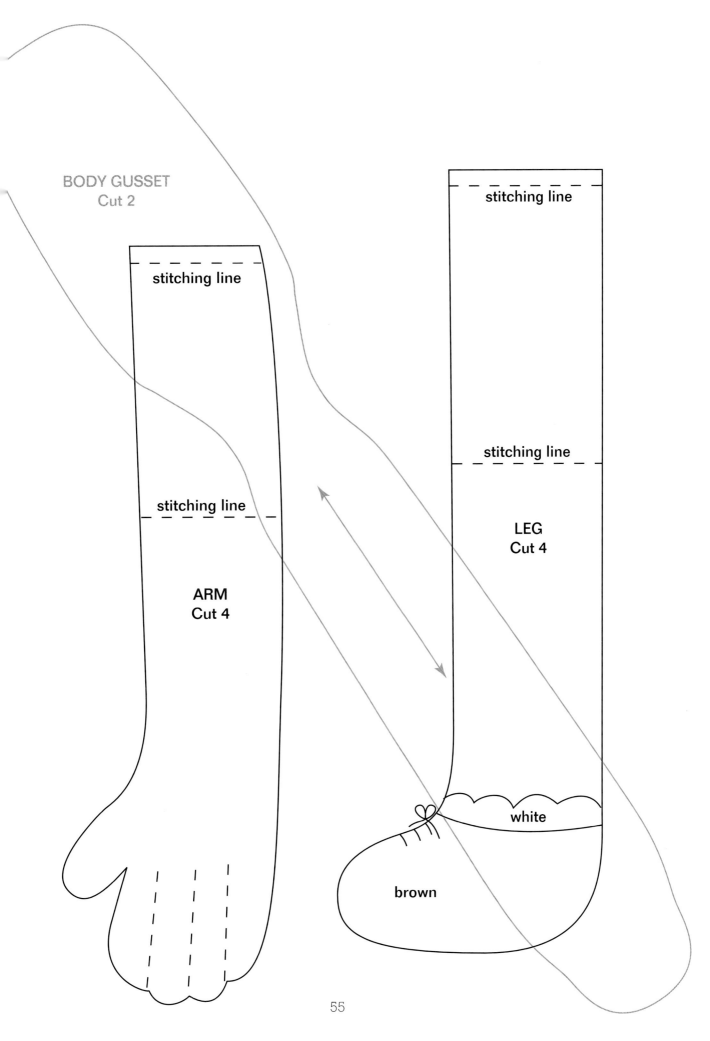

BODY GUSSET
Cut 2

stitching line

stitching line

ARM
Cut 4

stitching line

stitching line

LEG
Cut 4

white

brown

MARY-ANNE

By Susan York

Mary-Anne just loves her exquisite party dress, lavishly trimmed with lace. If only her guests would arrive soon!

SIZE

To fit a 46-51 cm (18-20 in) doll

MATERIALS

80 cm (31^1/$_2$ in) of 115 cm (45 in) wide voile or batiste

6.3 m (6^7/$_8$ yd) of 1 cm (^{3}/$_8$ in) wide insertion lace

30 cm (12 in) of beading

2 m (2^1/$_4$ yd) of 2 cm (^{3}/$_4$ in) wide lace edging

40 cm (16 in) of 1 cm (^{3}/$_8$ in) wide lace edging

1.2 m (1^1/$_3$ yd) of entredeux

Water-soluble pen or pencil

Tissue or tracing paper

Pencil

Fineline permanent marker pen

Matching sewing thread

Three small buttons

Small sharp scissors

BEFORE YOU BEGIN

See the patterns and lace-shaping designs on pages 59-61. All the seams are 1 cm (^{3}/$_8$ in). Trace all the patterns onto tissue or tracing paper, using the marker pen. Because of the lace-shaping on each piece of this dress, it is best to prepare each one prior to assembling the dress. Read all the instructions and the section on dressing dolls beginning on page 6.

CONSTRUCTION

FOR THE COLLAR

STEP ONE

Cut a 20 cm (8 in) square of fabric. Trace the lace-shaping design onto it, using the water-soluble pen or pencil.

STEP TWO

Carefully lay down Line 1 of the insertion lace, then lay down Line 2, pinning them both into place. Stitch them down with a small zigzag or hemstitch. Split the fabric behind the lace, taking care not to cut into the lace. Carefully cut away the fabric from behind the lace and the bottom layer of the doubled lace at the loops. Carefully cut away the fabric from around the outside edge of the collar.

STEP THREE

Gently gather 140 cm (55 in) of the 2 cm (^{3}/$_4$ in) wide lace edging. Sew the gathered lace around the edge of the collar using a small zigzag stitch.

STEP FOUR

Cut out the neckline on the collar, following the pattern line.

FOR THE SLEEVES

STEP ONE

Cut out two sleeves from the fabric. Trace the lace-shaping design onto each sleeve, using the water-soluble pen or pencil. Pin the insertion lace along the marked line, then stitch it down with a small zigzag or hemstitch. Split the fabric behind the lace, taking care not to cut into the lace. Carefully cut away the fabric from behind the lace and the bottom layer of the doubled lace at the loops.

STEP TWO

Gather the bottom edge of the sleeves, using two rows of small stitches. Pull up the gathering so the sleeve ends measure 12.5 cm (5 in). With the right sides facing, attach the insertion lace to the sleeve ends with a small straight stitch. Trim the fabric from the entredeux and trim the sleeve fabric to 3 mm (^{1}/$_8$ in). Neaten the seam with a small zigzag stitch.

STEP THREE

Trim the fabric from the other side of the entredeux, then attach a length of beading, using a small zigzag stitch.

STEP FOUR

For each sleeve, gently gather 25 cm (10 in) of the 2 cm (^{3}/$_4$ in) wide lace edging. Pull up the gathering so the lace edging fits the beading on the ends of the sleeves. Attach the lace edging with a small zigzag stitch.

STEP FIVE

Sew two rows of small gathering stitches along the sleeve heads, leaving the seam allowances free.

FOR THE SASHES

Cut a 7.5 cm (3 in) strip across the full width of the fabric. Cut the strip into

two equal lengths. Neaten both long sides and one end with a narrow rolled hem. Gather the other end to 12 mm ($^1/_2$ in). Set the sashes aside.

FOR THE BODICE

STEP ONE

Note that the left and right back bodices are self-facing because they have been cut on the fold. Fold each bodice piece along the centre back so the wrong sides are together and from now on treat them as a single piece. Join the shoulder seams of the front and back bodice with a small French seam.

STEP TWO

Pull up the gathering on the sleeve heads to fit the armholes. With the right sides together, pin, then stitch the sleeves into the armholes with a small straight stitch. Trim the seams and neaten with a zigzag stitch.

STEP THREE

Attach the sashes to the front bodice, 1 cm ($^3/_8$ in) above the waist.

STEP FOUR

Join the side and underarm seams in one go, using a small French seam, taking the sash ends into the seams.

STEP FIVE

Baste the collar into position. With the right sides together, stitch entredeux around the neck with a small straight stitch. Trim all the fabric and lace to 3 mm ($^1/_8$ in). Neaten the seam with zigzag stitching. Trim the fabric from the outer edge of the entredeux. Gently gather a length of the 1 cm ($^3/_8$ in) wide lace edging and attach it to the entredeux with small zigzag stitches.

STEP SIX

Attach a length of entredeux to the waist edge of the bodice.

FOR THE SKIRT

STEP ONE

Cut a piece of fabric 28-38 cm x 115 cm (11-15 in x 45 in). Note that the length will depend on the height of your doll. Mark the lace-shaping design onto the skirt, using the water-soluble pen or pencil so that the highest points are 15 cm (6 in) from the bottom edge of the skirt. Begin marking at the centre front; you should fit seven of the motifs around the skirt.

STEP TWO

Fold up a 7.5 cm (3 in) hem at the bottom edge of the skirt. Pin then attach the lace as for the bodice. Trim away the fabric and bottom layer of lace from the loops as for the bodice. Trim away the excess fabric at the hem.

STEP THREE

Beginning at the top edge, attach 9 cm ($3^1/_2$ in) of insertion lace on both sides of the skirt, using a small zigzag stitch to roll the fabric into the seam. Join the centre back seam of the skirt with a French seam, stitching through the bottom of the lace.

STEP FOUR

Gather the top edge of the skirt with three rows of stitches. Pull up the gathering so the skirt fits the bodice. Attach the skirt to the entredeux at the waist edge, using a small straight stitch. Trim the seam allowances to 3 mm ($^1/_8$ in) and neaten with a small zigzag stitch.

STEP FIVE

Make three small buttonholes and sew the buttons on to correspond.

Delicate lace shaping makes this beautiful collar

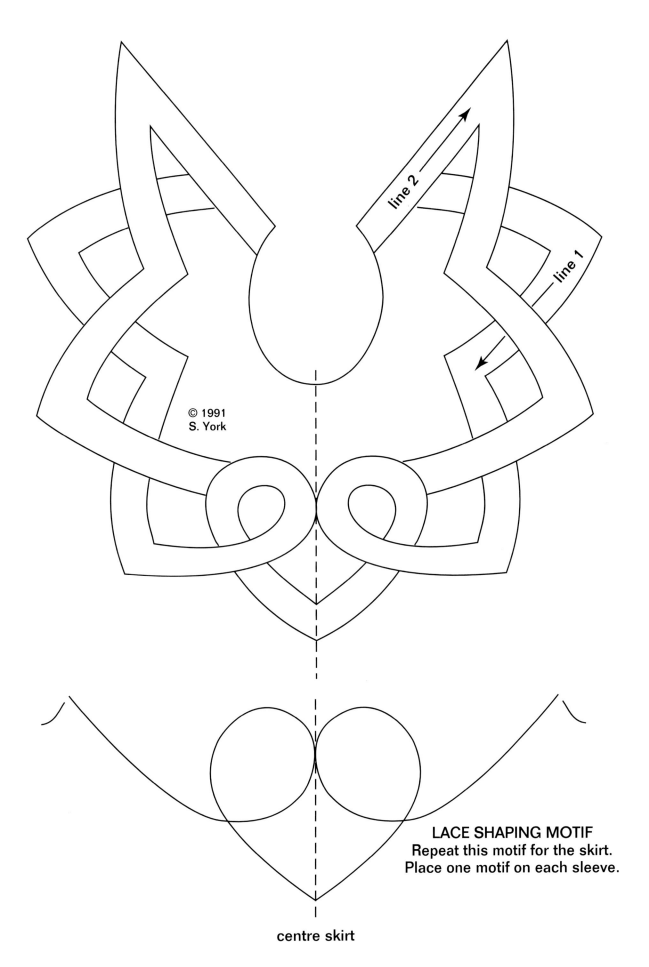

line 2

line 1

© 1991
S. York

LACE SHAPING MOTIF
Repeat this motif for the skirt.
Place one motif on each sleeve.

centre skirt

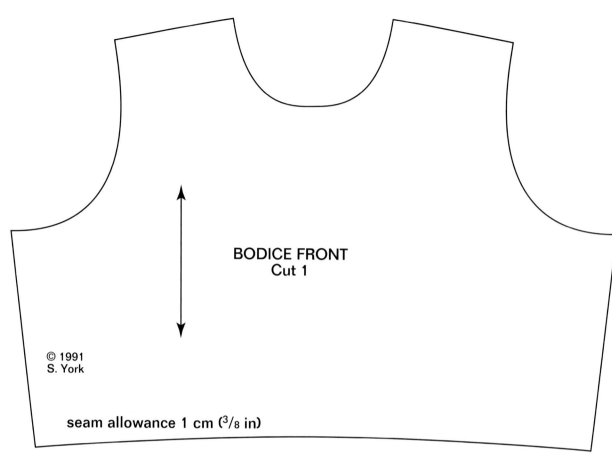

BODICE FRONT
Cut 1

© 1991
S. York

seam allowance 1 cm ($^3/_8$ in)

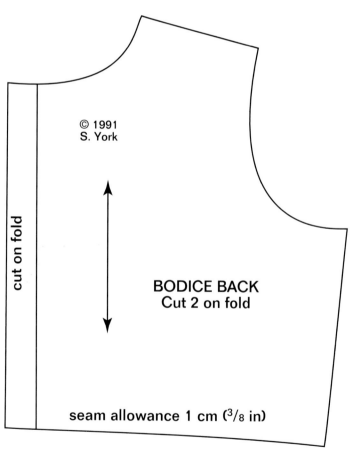

© 1991
S. York

cut on fold

BODICE BACK
Cut 2 on fold

seam allowance 1 cm ($^3/_8$ in)

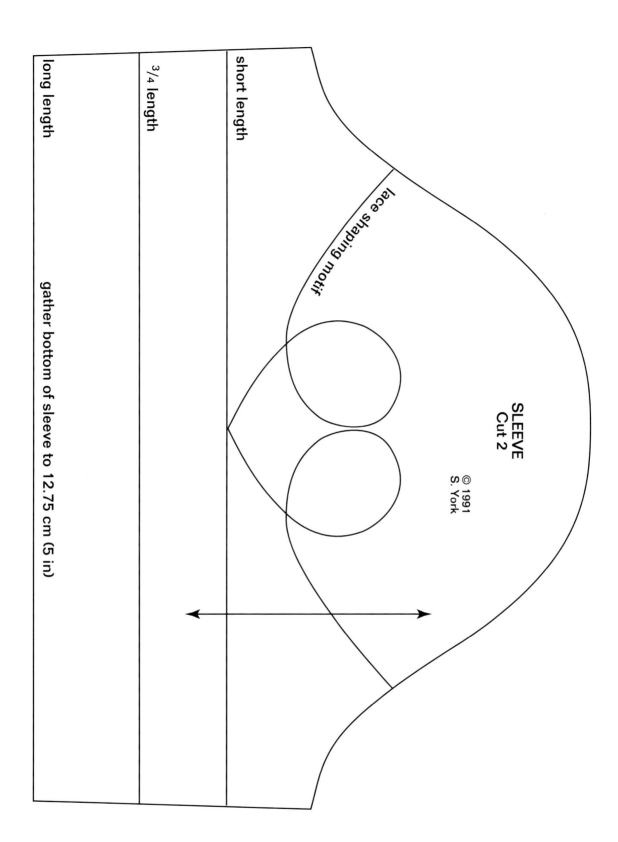

short length

3/4 length

long length

lace shaping motif

SLEEVE
Cut 2

© 1991
S. York

gather bottom of sleeve to 12.75 cm (5 in)

61

JUDITH

Well, it's back to school for young Judith who is all rugged up
against the cold in her smart woollen coat and beret.

SIZE

To fit 38 cm (15 in) doll

MATERIALS

For the overcoat
50 cm (19½ in) of Doctor flannel
50 cm (19½ in) of fabric for the lining
Eight buttons
Press studs (optional)
Water-soluble pen or pencil
Tissue or tracing paper
Fineline permanent marker pen
Matching sewing thread
For the beret
30 cm (12 in) of Doctor flannel
30 cm (12 in) of cotton lining
Small quantity of velvet ribbon

BEFORE YOU BEGIN

See the patterns on pages 65-67. All
the seams are 6 mm (¼ in). Read all the
instructions and the section on dressing dolls beginning on page 6. Trace
the pattern onto tissue or tracing
paper, using the marker pen.

CONSTRUCTION

STEP ONE

Note that the coat and the lining are
made separately, then joined. Using
the pattern provided, cut out all the
pattern pieces as directed for the coat
and the lining. Snip the corners where
indicated on the coat back and side
back, then join the back to the side

back pieces along the extensions. Fold
the pleats as marked. Baste across the
top of each pleat up to the slash to hold
the pleats in place, then stitch the short
underarm seams.

STEP TWO

Join the side backs to the fronts. Join the
shoulder seams.

STEP THREE

Make the lining up to this point in the
same way as for the coat. With the right
sides together, sew the front edge of
the lining to the front edge of the coat
facing. Press the coat front along the
fold line to create the facing.

FOR THE COLLAR

STEP ONE

Place the collar pieces together with
the right sides facing. Stitch around the
outer edge of the collar. Trim and clip
the corners and the curved seam
allowance. Turn the collar through to
the right side and press. Topstitch the
collar 6 mm (¼ in) from the edge.

STEP TWO

Match the centre of the collar to the
centre back. Pin and baste the collar
into position with both right sides
facing outwards. Pin the lining to neck
edge over the collar. With the right
sides facing stitch through all thick-
nesses to hold the collar in position.
Turn to the right side and trim the seam
allowance where necessary.

FOR THE SLEEVES

STEP ONE

Trim 6 mm (¼ in) from the bottom of
the sleeve lining. With the right sides
together, join the sleeve to the lining
across the bottom of the sleeve.

STEP TWO

Open out the sleeve and lining, then
sew the long sleeve seam of the coat
and of the lining in one go. Turn the
sleeve so that the lining is inside and
the sleeve heads match. Baste across
the sleeve heads and press. Gather the
sleeve heads to fit the armholes. Pin,
then stitch the sleeves into the armholes. Neaten the seams.

FOR THE BELT

Place the belt pieces together with the
right sides facing. Stitch around the
edge, leaving an opening on the long
side to turn through. Turn the belt to the
right side and slipstitch the opening
closed. Topstitch around the belt. Hold
the belt in place on the coat with a
button at either end.

FOR THE HEM

Turn up 1 cm (½ in) hem (or whatever
is required for your doll). Hem the coat
and lining separately for a better finish.

TO COMPLETE

Fit the coat on the doll and overlap the fronts as suits. Mark the placement for six buttons. You can make three buttonholes or use press studs under the buttons. We chose the latter.

BERET

STEP ONE

Cut a circle with a radius of 13 cm (5 in) from the flannel and from the lining. Cut a 2.5 cm (1 in) wide strip of flannel the length of the circumference of the doll's head plus 12 mm (¹/₂ in).

STEP TWO

Using a 6 mm (¹/₄ in) seam, join the short ends of the strip to form a loop. Press the seam open. Press 6 mm (¹/₄ in) to the wrong side on one raw edge of the loop. Divide the length of the loop into quarters and mark with pins.

STEP THREE

Baste the two circles together with the wrong sides facing. Mark the quarter points around the edge of the circle.

Gather around the edge of the circle with two rows of gathering stitches. Pull up the gathering to fit the loop. With the right sides facing, stitch the raw edge of the loop to the circle matching quarter points. Slipstitch the pressed edge of the loop to the inside of the beret over the previous stitching. Make a small bow from the velvet ribbon and slipstitch it to the front of the beret.

A belt and pleat detail add a trim tailored look

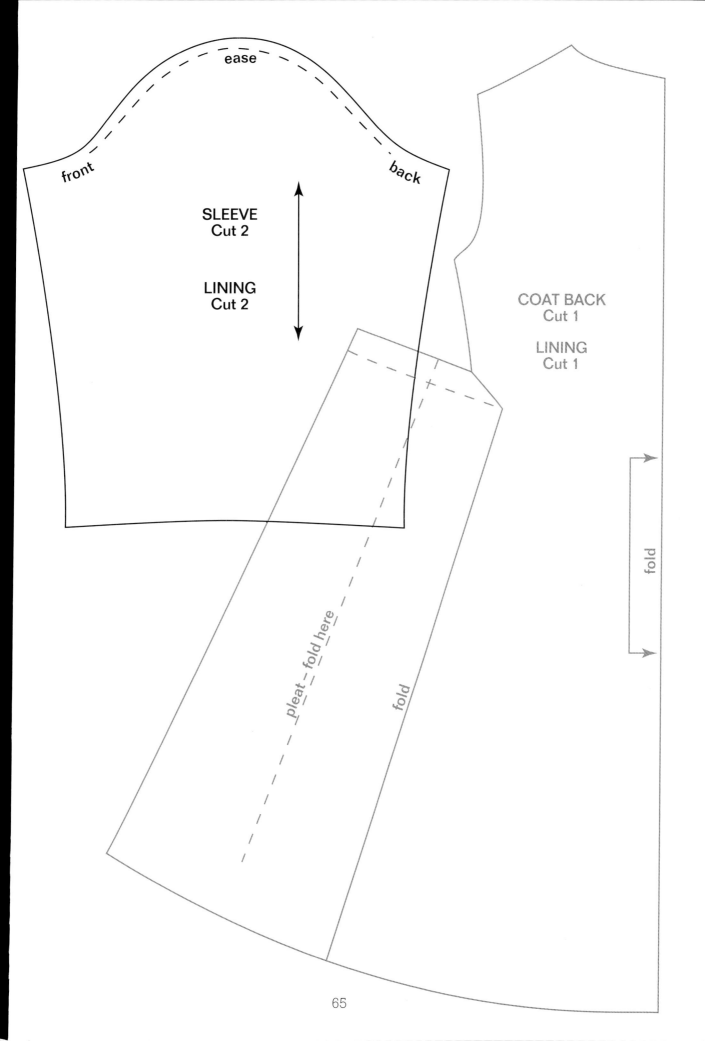

ease

front

back

SLEEVE
Cut 2

LINING
Cut 2

COAT BACK
Cut 1

LINING
Cut 1

pleat - fold here

fold

fold

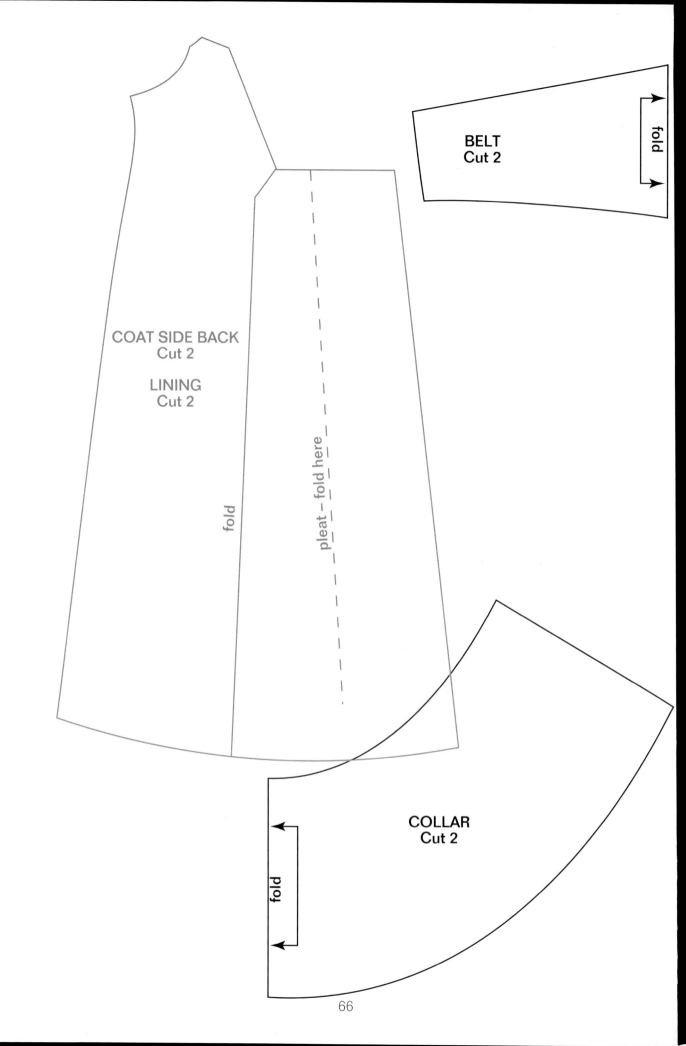

BELT
Cut 2

fold

COAT SIDE BACK
Cut 2

LINING
Cut 2

fold

pleat – fold here

COLLAR
Cut 2

fold

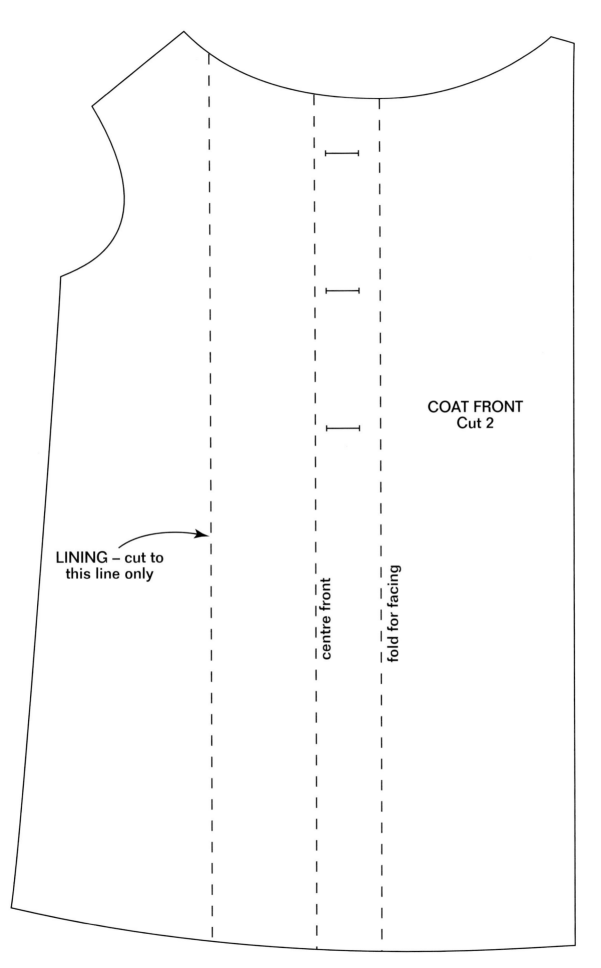

COAT FRONT
Cut 2

LINING – cut to
this line only

centre front

fold for facing

TATIANA

By Anne's Glory Box

**With her basket overflowing with
fresh-picked fruit, Tatiana enjoys a moment's
rest on the way to her home.**

SIZE

Finished size: 88 cm (34½ in)

MATERIALS

30 cm (12 in) of fabric for the body
   and skirt
20 cm (8 in) of fabric for the arms
   and the head
20 cm (8 in) of fabric for the legs
10 cm (4 in) of fabric for the face
20 cm (8 in) of fabric for the skirt
   overlay and knickers
60 cm (24 in) of 5 cm (2 in) wide
   crocheted lace
6 mm (¼ in) wide elastic
Two buttons
Sakura Micro Pigma fabric pens:
   Black, Sepia, Green, Red
Polyester fibre fill

BEFORE YOU BEGIN

See the patterns on pages 70-71. All
the seams are 6 mm (¼ in). Read all the
instructions and the section on making
cloth dolls on page 12.

CONSTRUCTION

FOR THE SKIRT

STEP ONE

Cut a 37 cm x 61 cm (14½ in x 24 in)
piece from the skirt fabric. Cut a

12.5 cm x 61 cm (5 in x 24 in) piece
from the overlay fabric.

STEP TWO

Sew a 6 mm (¼ in) hem on one long
side of the overlay. With the right sides
facing, place the overlay on the skirt
with the top edges matching. Stitch
them together 9 cm (3½ in) from the
top edge. Turn the overlay down.

STEP THREE

Turn under 6 mm (¼ in) on the bottom
of the skirt, then turn another 2.5 cm
(1 in). Stitch the hem, then press.

STEP FOUR

Fold the skirt to be 37 cm x 30.5 cm
(14½ in x 12 in). Stitch the centre back
seam.

STEP FIVE

At the top edge of the skirt, turn under
6 mm (¼ in), then turn under 2.5 cm
(1 in) to form a casing. Stitch, then press.

FOR THE LEGS

Using the pattern provided, cut out
four legs from the appropriate fabric.
Using a 6 mm (¼ in) seam allowance
and small machine stitches, sew the
legs together in pairs, with the right
sides facing. Clip the seam allowances,
then turn the legs to the right side. Fill
firmly up to the knees. With the feet
facing to the front, stitch across at the
knees, then continue stuffing the legs
up to 2.5 cm (1 in) from the top. Stitch
across the legs at this point.

FOR THE KNICKERS

STEP ONE

Cut two pieces of fabric, each 19 cm
24 cm (7½ in x 9½ in). Turn up a 6 mm
(¼ in) hem on one bottom edge o
each piece. Stitch a length of lace ove
the hem.

STEP TWO

Fold each piece over double, length
wise, with the right sides facing. Stitch
the long side on each one. Turn the
tubes to the right side and pull one
over each leg so the top edges and the
back seams are matching.

FOR THE BODY

STEP ONE

Using the pattern provided, cut two
body pieces on the fold and two arm
pieces. With the right sides facing, sew
one arm to each side of both body
pieces, taking care that the arm pieces
are matching. Place the two body/arm
pieces together with the right sides
facing, sew around the sides and the
arms, leaving the neck and bottom
edges open.

STEP TWO

Fill the body and arms firmly up to
12 mm (½ in) from the bottom. Turn
under 12 mm (½ in) at the bottom. Slip
the top of the legs inside the body.

Stitch across the bottom edge of the body, securing the legs.

FOR THE HEAD

STEP ONE

Using the pattern provided, cut two head pieces. Staystitch around the face edge of both pieces to prevent stretching. Place the head pieces together with the right sides facing. Stitch from **A** to **B** and from **C** to **D**.

STEP TWO

With the right sides facing, carefully stitch the face into position, matching the notches on the face to the seams on the head. Stuff the head firmly, taking care that the face remains flat.

STEP THREE

Using the Pigma pens, draw in the facial features as follows: outline the eyebrows in Sepia, then Black; outline the eyes in Sepia, then Black; colour the irises Green and add a Black pupil; outline the lips in Sepia, colour in in Red; outline the cheeks with a dotted Red line and cross-hatch lightly in Red.

STEP FOUR

Fit the neck into the body opening, then stitch it in place.

TO COMPLETE

STEP ONE

Wrap a length of lace around the doll's shoulders, gathering it at the back to shape it.

STEP TWO

Cut a length of elastic to fit the doll's waist. Thread the elastic through the casing on the skirt and secure the ends. Pull the skirt on to the doll, over the ends of the shawl.

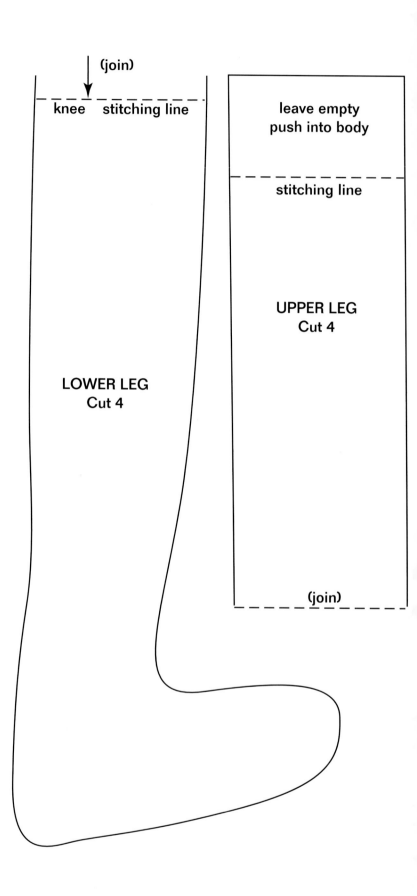

(join)

knee   stitching line

leave empty
push into body

stitching line

UPPER LEG
Cut 4

LOWER LEG
Cut 4

(join)

70

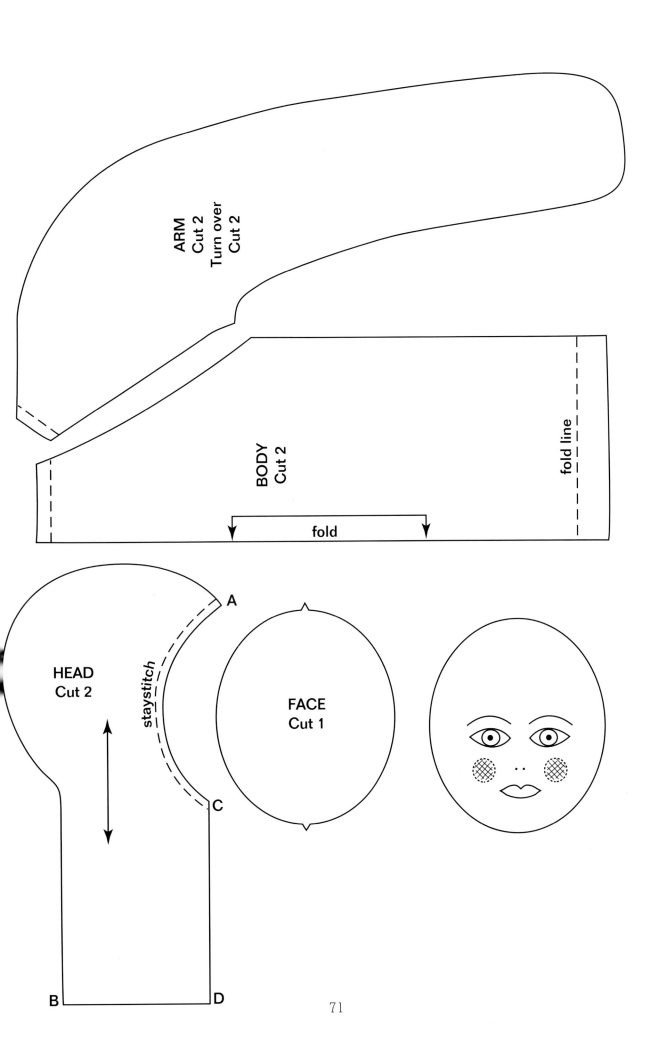

ARM
Cut 2
Turn over
Cut 2

BODY
Cut 2

fold line

fold

A

HEAD
Cut 2

staystitch

C

FACE
Cut 1

B   D

71

PATRICIA

By Anne's Glory Box

**Why does it always rain just as you're ready to leave?
Patricia waits in the conservatory for the sun to return.**

Patricia's elegant bonnet is available from Marie Viazam, phone (02) 558 2997.

SIZE

To fit a 53 cm (21 in) lady doll

MATERIALS

25 cm (10 in) of Thai silk for the skirt and the dicky
25 cm (10 in) of fabric for the jacket
10 cm (4 in) of wide lace for the dicky
Press studs
Small amount of tulle
Matching sewing threads
Tissue or tracing paper
Fineline permanent marker pen

BEFORE YOU BEGIN

See the patterns on pages 74-76. Note that the skirt pattern is given in parts. Join them from **A-B** and **C-D** before cutting out fabric. All the seams are 6 mm (¹/₄ in). Read all the instructions and the section on dressing dolls beginning on page 6. Trace the pattern onto tissue or tracing paper, using the marker pen.

CONSTRUCTION

FOR THE JACKET

STEP ONE

Using the pattern provided, cut out the pattern pieces as instructed. Stitch the darts in the jacket back and the lining. Stitch the shoulder and side seams of the jacket and of the lining.

STEP TWO

With the right sides together, join the jacket to the lining right around the edges. Turn the jacket through to the right side through the armholes.

STEP THREE

Gather the sleeve heads to fit the armholes. Stitch a 3 mm (¹/₈ in) hem on the sleeve ends. Stitch the underarm seams. Pin, then stitch the sleeves into the armholes. Press the lapels along the fold line marked on the pattern.

FOR THE DICKY

STEP ONE

Using the pattern provided, cut out the pattern pieces as instructed. Pin the dicky and lining together with the right sides facing. Stitch around the edges, leaving a small opening on one side. Turn through to the right side and press.

STEP TWO

Trim the lace to the same width as the dicky, then attach the lace to the dicky at the sides. Carefully handstitch the dicky to the inside of the jacket front on the right-hand side. Sew small press studs on the left-hand side to close the jacket front.

FOR THE SKIRT

STEP ONE

Using the pattern provided, cut out the pattern pieces as instructed. Stitch the darts in the skirt front.

STEP TWO

Cut a piece of tulle 12.7 cm (5 in) long and as wide as three-quarters of the width of the skirt back. Fold the tulle in half. Baste the tulle onto the wrong side of the skirt back at the waistband, then gather the two together to fit the back of the doll.

STEP THREE

Stitch the side seams of the skirt, leaving an opening on one side to fit the skirt onto the doll. Measure the doll's waist, then cut a 2.5 cm (1 in) wide band to fit. Sew one edge of the waistband to the skirt, with the right sides together. Turn in the ends and fold the waistband over double to the inside. Turn under the raw edge and slipstitch it over the seam. Neaten the edges of the opening by hand. Sew on a press stud to close the skirt. Turn in 3 mm (¹/₈ in), then turn another 12 mm (¹/₂ in) for the hem. Hand-stitch the hem.

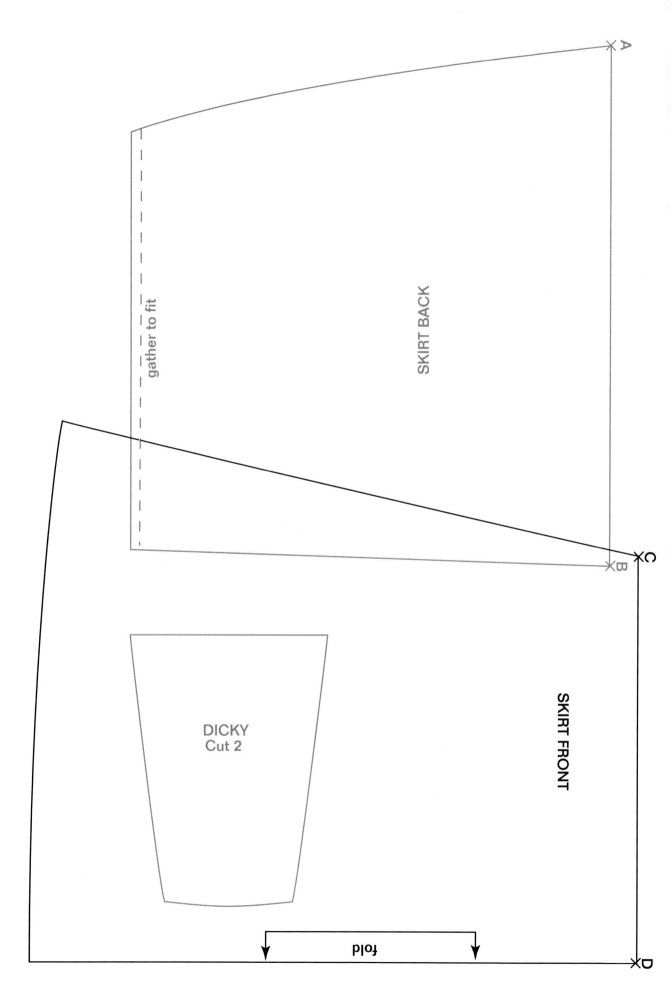

A

gather to fit

SKIRT BACK

B
C

DICKY
Cut 2

SKIRT FRONT

fold

D

74

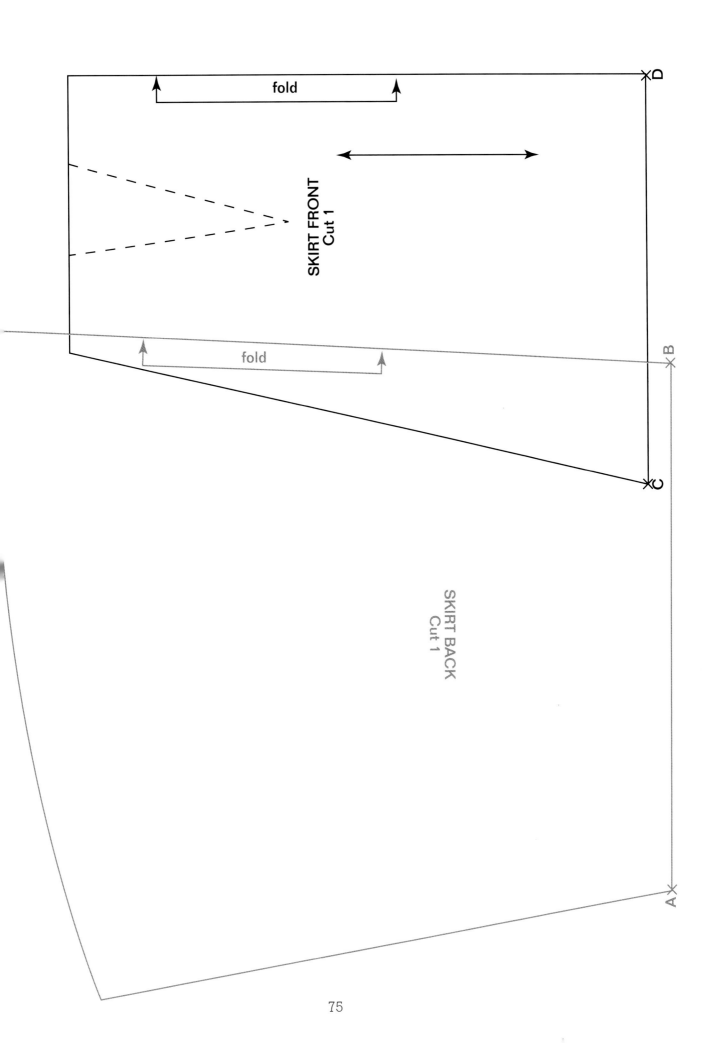

fold

SKIRT FRONT
Cut 1

fold

B

C

D

SKIRT BACK
Cut 1

A

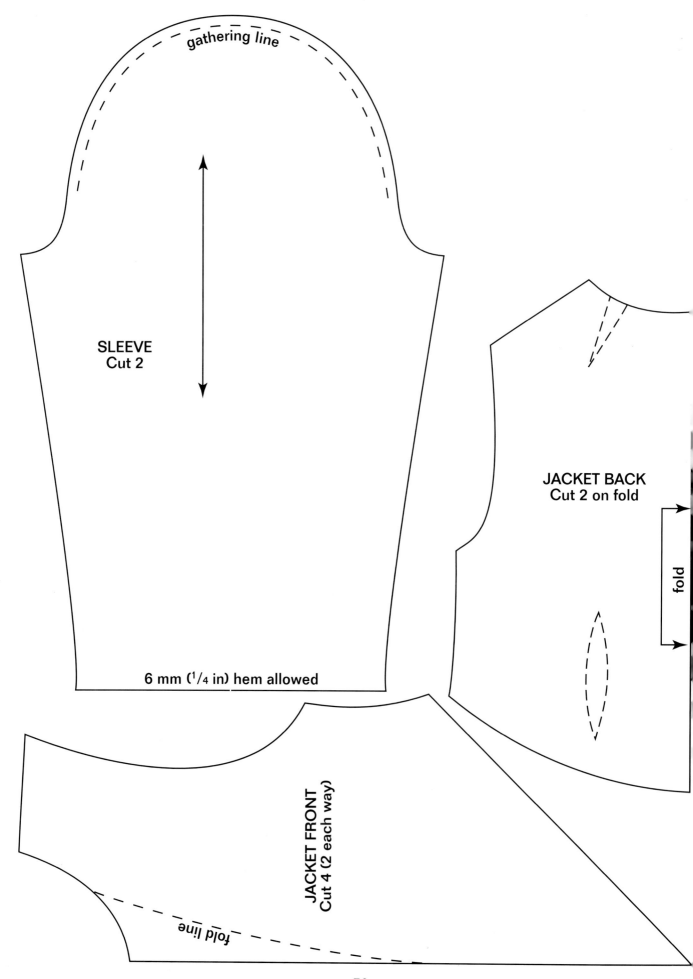

gathering line

SLEEVE
Cut 2

6 mm (¹/₄ in) hem allowed

JACKET BACK
Cut 2 on fold

fold

JACKET FRONT
Cut 4 (2 each way)

fold line

JACQUELINE

By Anne's Glory Box

Lost in contemplation of the paintings, Jacqueline
reflects on the beauty around her.

SIZE

To fit a 38 cm (15 in) doll

MATERIALS

For the dress
40 cm (16 in) of Thai silk
2.4 m (2²/₃ yd) of 12 mm (¹/₂ in) wide
   flat braid
For the bonnet
25 cm (10 in) of Thai silk
20 cm (8 in) of buckram
2 m (2¹/₄ yd) of double-edge lace
30 cm (12 in) of braid
1.5 m (1²/₃ yd) of 4 mm (³/₁₆ in) wide
   silk ribbon
Two silk roses

BEFORE YOU BEGIN

See the patterns on pages 78 and 80.
All the seams are 6 mm (¹/₄ in). Read all
the instructions and the section on
dressing dolls beginning on page 6.

CONSTRUCTION

FOR THE SKIRT

STEP ONE

Cut a piece of Thai silk 20 cm x 47 cm
(8 in x 18¹/₂ in). On one long side, turn
up 6 mm (¹/₄ in), then turn another
2.5 cm (1 in). Stitch the hem, then press.
Stitch a row of braid over the stitching.

Stitch on a second row of braid 12 mm
(¹/₂ in) above the first row.

STEP TWO

Across the raw long side, mark every
2.5 cm (1 in). Pleat the skirt by bringing
the first mark to the second, the third
mark to the fourth and so on right
across the width. Baste the pleats in
place across the top edge of the skirt.

STEP THREE

Measure the doll's waist. Cut a waistband to this measurement and 2.5 cm
(1 in) wide. With the right sides facing,
stitch one side of the waistband to the
skirt, easing the pleats to fit.

STEP FOUR

Sew the centre back seam of the skirt
and waistband up to 5 cm (2 in) from
the top. Turn under 6 mm (¹/₄ in) on the
free side of the waistband, then fold the
waistband over double. Stitch the free
side down over the previous stitching.

**The matching bonnet features
pleated lace and braid**

FOR THE TOP

STEP ONE

Using the pattern provided, cut out one
front and two backs and the neck
facings as instructed on the pattern.
Sew the shoulder seams of the top and
of the facings.

STEP TWO

With the right sides facing, pin the neck
facing to the top, matching raw neck
edges. Stitch around the neck edge.
Trim and clip the seam. Turn the facing
to the inside and press.

STEP THREE

On the back opening, neaten the raw
edges, then turn in 3 mm (¹/₈ in) and
stitch the edges down.

STEP FOUR

Cut out two sleeves. Turn up a small
hem on the sleeve ends. Stitch on a row
of braid to cover the hem stitching.
Gather the sleeve heads. Pin and stitch
the sleeves into the armholes. Sew the
side and underarm seams in one continuous seam.

STEP FOUR

Turn up a small hem at the bottom
edge. Sew on a row of braid over the
stitching as for the sleeves.

FOR THE COLLAR

STEP ONE

With the right sides facing, stitch the neck edge of the collar pieces. Turn the collar to the right side and press well. Neaten the outer edge of the collar with a small zigzag stitch, then stitch a row of braid around the collar.

STEP TWO

Lay the collar in place over the top. Arrange three rows of braid to fit in the V-shaped opening and stitch them in place. Catch the collar to the front of the top with a few small stitches.

BONNET

STEP ONE

Cut out a circle 7 cm (2³⁄₄ in) in diameter and using the pattern provided, cut a brim from the buckram. Clip all around the circle at 6 mm (¹⁄₄ in) intervals. Overlap the ends of the buckram brim to the marked lines and stitch.

STEP TWO

Beginning at the join, back-stitch the brim to the circle, stitching 6 mm (¹⁄₄ in) from the edge. Stitch the darts in the brim as marked on the pattern.

STEP THREE

Using the pattern provided, cut out the bonnet fabric. Fold and press the darts as marked. Pin the fabric into position over the buckram, then hand-stitch to secure it.

STEP FOUR

Pleat 1 m (1¹⁄₈ yd) of lace to fit across the outside of the brim. Hand-stitch it in place. Hand-stitch a length of lace to the inside of the brim and around the back inside edge of the bonnet. Stitch a length of braid over the stitching on the pleated lace. Attach a rose and a length of ribbon to each side.

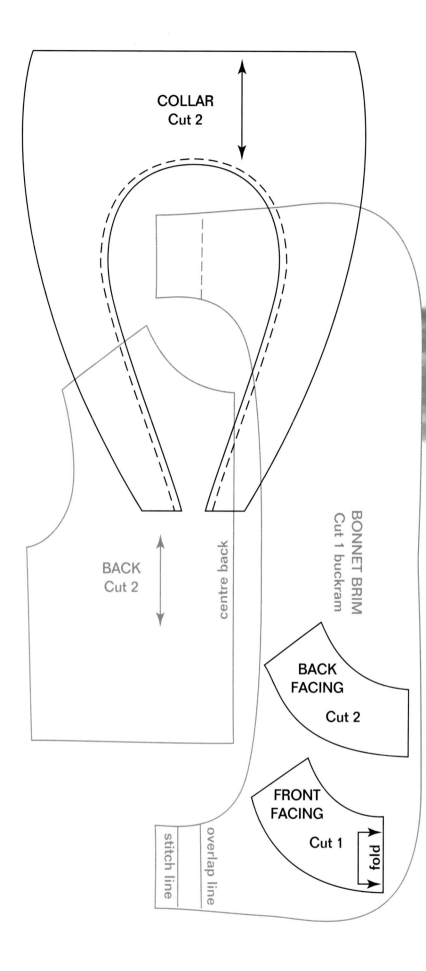

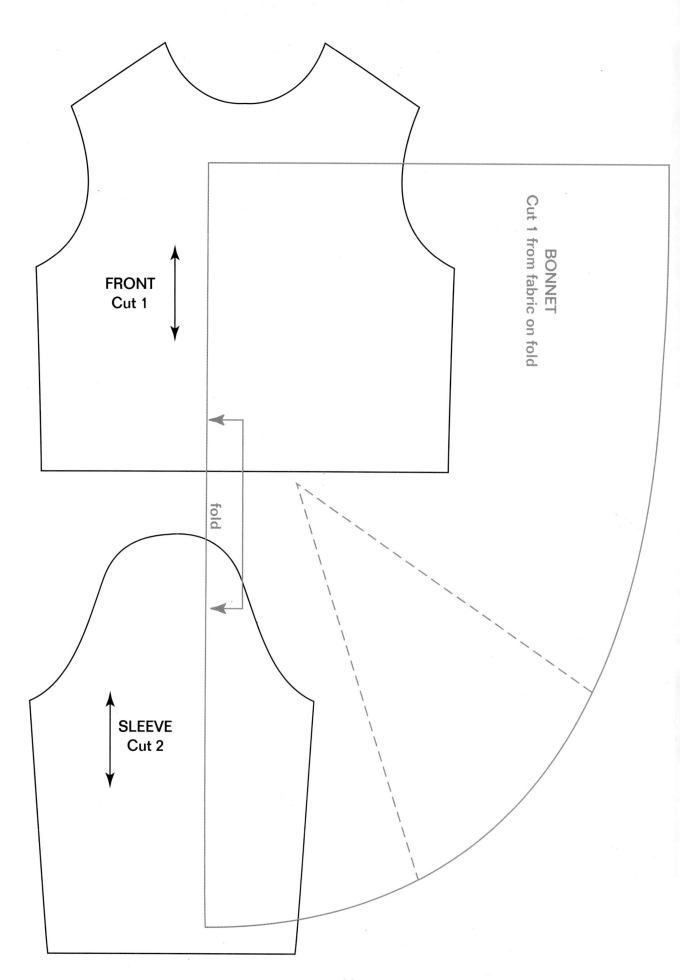

FRONT
Cut 1

SLEEVE
Cut 2

BONNET
Cut 1 from fabric on fold

fold